Between Shadow and Light: The Work of Maryann Thompson

Caroline Constant
with contributions by Shantel Blakely, Terry Real, and Doug Reed

Introduction

Maryann Thompson, as one of her clients declared, inhabits "a liminal space, a threshold"—a space of both-and, of inside and outside, of shadow and light.[1] She occupies a dialogic space, a position from which to examine a situation from multiple perspectives, to facilitate opportunities for discussion, and, ultimately, to seek a consensual basis for design. The innovative qualities of Thompson's work derive from this process of negotiating difference in which the voices of the various participants are of strategic importance. In *The Situation and the Story*, essayist Vivian Gornick explains the effect that results from such reciprocal relationships: "The story here was not either the speaker or the doctor per se; it was what happened to each of them in the other's company."[2]

For Thompson, architecture is the stage on which we live our lives, a philosophy that foregrounds architecture's inherent symbolism, its ability to arouse our emotions, to challenge our preconceptions, and to provide sites of individual solace and respite from quotidian affairs, as well as of heightened collective interaction. Her inclusive design process encompasses extended conversations with clients, patrons, users, and ultimately with the public at large—each interaction a means to address the collective social dimension of the work. Integral to this process is collaboration, which assumes various forms: among the staff members of her firm Maryann Thompson Architects (MTA); with professionals from related disciplines; with professionals who are integral to the client base (for example, scientists in the case of the Broad Institute); and with the community of users, including the client.

Thompson's process of establishing priorities and aspirations for a design begins with the extensive questionnaires that she formulates for her clients and their associates. Responses are solicited from every family member in the case of a private residence, from students and janitorial staff, faculty, administrators, alumni, and parents in the case of an educational facility, and from civic or institutional leaders as well as interested members of the public in the case of work for philanthropic organizations or commissions in the public realm. Thought-provoking questions probe such issues as institutional or family values, the time of day spent in a certain type of space, or the desired quality of natural light and views. The results are compiled in a document that takes the form of a novella in which each participant is given a voice, however varied the opinions might be. To address the visual basis of this collaborative process, Thompson draws upon an iterative method she borrowed from her early collaborators Doug Reed and Gary Hilderbrand, which they term a "char-

1 Meera Viswanathan, Head of Ethel Walker School, in conversation with Maryann Thompson, October 2022. Architect Robert Venturi brought the phrase "both-and" to prominence in architectural discourse with his "gentle manifesto," *Complexity and Contradiction in Architecture* (1966). Seeking to counter the "tradition of 'either-or'" that he associated with orthodox modern architecture, Venturi encouraged architects to consider the potential for ambiguity in architectural form which, among other virtues, would engage the observer more actively in acts of interpretation. See Robert Venturi, *Complexity and Contradiction in Architecture* (New York: Museum of Modern Art, 1966), 30–31.

2 Vivian Gornick, *The Situation and the Story: The Art of Personal Narrative* (New York: Farrar, Straus and Giroux, 2001), 5–6.

acter study." Clients are periodically asked to respond quickly and instinctively to a set of flash cards to elicit their emotional, intuitive responses to relevant images. The initial sets might focus on abstract issues of form or relative amounts of light or darkness. Subsequent examples engage more particular aesthetic proclivities, while those used during design development are directed to details such as materials and finishes.

The satisfaction that derives from the various methods by which Thompson facilitates her clients' agency in the design process is borne out by the significant number of her firm's repeat commissions—a vacation house followed by a principal residence, or a house followed by office space, for example. Of particular note are the numerous projects that she has carried out with the landscape architecture firm Michael Van Valkenburgh Associates (MVVA). These are emblematic not only of Van Valkenburgh's interest in emancipating landscape architecture from its traditional subsidiary relationship to architecture but also of Thompson's concern for developing an architecture that is deferential to the conditions of its site.

Van Valkenburgh played a decisive role in Thompson's professional development, initially as a professor of landscape architecture when she was a student in several of his courses at Harvard's Graduate School of Design (GSD). Following completion of her professional degrees in architecture and landscape architecture in 1989, Thompson worked in Van Valkenburgh's Cambridge office while taking on a series of independent projects with her future partner Charles Rose. The commission to design a studio complex for the Atlantic Center of the Arts in New Smyrna Beach, Florida (1989–97) prompted the pair to launch their firm, Thompson and Rose Architects in Cambridge in 1991. The dissolution of their partnership in 2000 led Thompson to assume responsibility for several of the firm's projects, which provided fundamental starting points for themes she continues to develop in her independent practice. These include two designs in which the integration of architecture and landscape was critical: the Leventritt Garden Pavilion in the Boston Arboretum (with Reed Hilderbrand, 1997–2002) and the Visitor Center at the Polly Hill Arboretum (with MVVA, 1999–2001).

Thompson's distinctive approach to practice also derives from the value she places on teaching as a vehicle for developing her own voice, while simultaneously opening herself to new ways of thinking. As a part-time visiting critic in landscape architecture (1994–99) and as Professor in Practice of Architecture (2002–17) at the GSD, she pursued a dialogic approach to teaching in which students' vantage points are respected. The instructor operates as a facilitator, encouraging students to build on their own and each other's ideas. She likens the experience of engaging with the variety of opinions and range of expertise among her GSD students and colleagues to familial relations and their mode of interaction to that in an agora, which arose as a site of civic discourse for the ancient Greeks before it was used as a marketplace. At the same time, she seeks to counter certain pedagogic principles that were then being promulgated in design schools: a focus on the beauty of the image or the distinctive qualities of a singular object as a mark of invention or innovation, the priority given to parametric design, and the detachment that results from an exclusive reliance on computer-based representation—all to the detriment of the ways in which a work of architecture might be experienced. Thompson accordingly affirms the role of freehand drawing as a means to probe the experiential dimension of architecture and its value as an art form with significant cultural and environmental implications. Toward that end, she seeks to cultivate drawing skills among the members of her office staff by scheduling weekly sketching sessions with live models—a practice that was interrupted by the Covid-19 restrictions of 2020–22.

Figure 1 Maryann Thompson, sketch study of section, Visitor Center, Polly Hill Arboretum, West Tisbury (drawing c. 2000)

The MTA office is administered in a manner loosely inspired by that in a typical graduate school design studio. While Thompson sets the agenda for the projects based on initial meetings with the clients and sketches made during early site visits, she works with the various project managers to develop alternate site and building strategies and refine each design. As a scheme gains greater specificity, MTA principal Martha Foss and senior associate Zac Cardwell are brought in to ensure that the design conforms with code requirements and the best construction practices, and they check every drawing set to ensure that technical details are appropriately resolved. Critical feedback on the work in progress is solicited at weekly meetings in which the project managers present the status of each project and the entire MTA team is brought into the conversation. These become teaching moments for the staff as well as means to clarify and further the design intentions.

The structure of this book emerged gradually over the course of a series of conversations that began during the long, dark Covid-19 lockdown in winter 2020–21. While they provided a respite from the uncertainty brought on by the global pandemic, these weekly meetings were a vehicle for Thompson and I to probe our mutual interest in the interrelationship of architecture and landscape architecture and the ways in which this theme is manifested in the work. Although certain projects were on hold for fundraising during this period, new commissions continued to arise at a welcome pace, keeping Thompson, her associates, and staff members busy with Zoom meetings.

From the outset of this effort, neither the evolution of Thompson's practice nor a strict programmatic approach to the work seemed to provide an adequate framework for addressing the ways in which certain prominent themes transcend notions of chronological development or typological classification. Consider, for example, the way in which Thompson imbues such diverse examples as park structures, scientific laboratories, and restaurants with qualities of inhabitation or gathering. The book's tripartite organization begins with a set of essays on certain theoretical starting points; this is followed by an elaboration of distinctive architectural themes, and it ends with a discussion of selected examples of the work, classified according to the type of building program. An interview with Thompson is followed by an appendix, which includes project credits compiled by Martha Foss as well as a selected bibliography.

It quickly became clear that other voices were needed to convey the ways in which Thompson works with her collaborators and clients. Only they could elaborate upon the experience of living in her houses or principles gleaned from working in her firm. Our inquiries to her client and frequent collaborator, landscape architect Doug Reed, to her residential client, family therapist Terry Real, and to a former member of Thompson's staff, architectural historian Shantel Blakely, were greeted with enthusiasm. Although no restrictions were placed on the nature of their contributions, each fit neatly within the book's organization as it evolved, and they provide important insights into the reciprocal nature of the process, affording a glimpse into "what happened to each of them in the other's company."

Part I Essays

Architecture as a Form of Mediation in the Natural World

A prominent feature of Maryann Thompson's professional contribution derives from her interest in the interrelationship of architecture and the natural world. This theme is particularly germane to her designs for a series of park pavilions, visitor centers, educational venues, and recreational facilities, among other programmatic types. All are directed to enhancing the communal potential of their locales—and in certain examples the historic significance of their sites. In each case the building is subsidiary to its environs, reflecting Thompson's understanding of the natural realm as a resource to be conserved on spiritual as well as environmental grounds. Architecture, then, is a vehicle for conveying such values to the public.

Thompson traces her interest in the spiritual value of nature to her youth spent in the Ohio countryside, when she lived on a horse farm outside Cincinnati. She began to appreciate the potential for integrating architecture and landscape design during numerous trips with her father to Columbus, Indiana, where she was particularly drawn to Daniel Kiley's contributions to the architectural projects commissioned by the town's benefactor, J. Irwin Miller. After completing her undergraduate degree in architecture at Princeton University and embarking on graduate studies at Columbia University, Thompson sought a more interdisciplinary approach. She enrolled at Harvard's Graduate School of Design during a propitious period in that institution's evolution when mutual interests were a focus of conversations among a trio of junior faculty members, which included myself in architecture and Mirka Beneš and Elizabeth Meyer in landscape architecture. Professor Michael Van Valkenburgh's course on plants—their habits, growth, and the subtlety of their coloring as they undergo seasonal variation—was a further source of inspiration. After earning Master's degrees in architecture and landscape architecture in 1989, Thompson worked in Van Valkenburgh's office for two years while undertaking independent commissions with Charles Rose. They launched their own firm, Thompson and Rose Architects, in 1991, and quickly became known for their site strategies, which reflect the integration of architecture and landscape, as well as for their building designs. Since founding her independent practice Maryann Thompson Architects (MTA) in 2000, Thompson continues to pursue the means to achieve such integration in her architectural commissions, which she frequently carries out in collaboration with landscape architects.

Figure 2 Leventritt Garden Pavilion, Arnold Arboretum, Boston, view from southeast

Leventritt Garden Pavilion, Arnold Arboretum, Boston, MA, with Reed Hilderbrand (1997–2002)

Thompson's open-air pavilion for the Leventritt Garden at Harvard University's Arnold Arboretum epitomizes her conception of architecture as an art form that weaves a dialogue between forms of human manufacture and those that derive from natural rhythms of growth and decay. [Fig. 2] The commission stemmed from her collaboration with landscape architects Doug Reed and Gary Hilderbrand, who invited Thompson to participate in the design competition for the garden. The team's winning entry prompted Reed and Hilderbrand to launch their own professional partnership in 1997.

As an adjunct to the historic Arnold Arboretum, founded in 1872 for "the promotion of Agricultural or Horticultural improvements," the Leventritt Garden occupies the northernmost segment of the botanical garden's research facilities in a portion of the original Adams Institution Grounds. It abuts the Dana Greenhouses (1963), where new plants are introduced, either grown from seed or propagated from cuttings. As a working landscape, the Leventritt Garden not only supports the Arboretum's general research agenda of tracing the evolution and biology of woody plants but also enables visitors to experience the growth, habit, and culture of the garden's one hundred-fifty species of woody shrubs and vines.

Thompson's pavilion occupies the westernmost corner of the triangular three-acre site, which Reed Hilderbrand terraced to reconcile the need for solar access with the thirty-foot grade change of its northeastern-facing slope. Her design amplifies the sequence of discovery and disclosure

1. Pedestrian Approach
2. Vine - Covered Trellises
3. Grass Lawn
4. Pavilion

that characterizes their garden layout, which in turn draws upon the Arboretum's existing circulation system and spatial patterns as laid out by Frederick Law Olmsted and elaborated by the Arboretum's first director—the botanist Charles Sprague Sargent. The principal pedestrian approach follows the course of a reconstructed stream bed. It affords distant views of the pavilion's skewed roof planes, which soar above the vine-covered trellises that line the pathway and signal the garden as a destination. [Figs. 3 & 4] Thompson devised the system of stainless steel trellises to punctuate an unfolding sequence of framed views to the terraces below, which coalesce around a central lawn that extends the full length of the garden. Just beyond the lawn is the pavilion, which sits at the head of the final set of terraces. The approach route terminates in a wooden bench at its western edge, which lines a freestanding stone wall that blocks the traffic noise from a nearby street.

Thompson conceived of the pavilion's structure as a system of supports that contributes in a didactic manner to the expressive purpose of the movement sequence. The columnar grid aligns with the final set of trellises. It is skewed so that views into the pavilion are veiled from the approach, then dramatically open to the garden from within its elevated position above the terraces. To compensate for the pavilion's northeastern orientation, Thompson split its roof into a pair of inclined planes to provide the space below with a degree of direct solar exposure through the gap between them. [See Fig. 134] The angles of the roofs echo those of the planting beds and the columns, transposing the earth forms skyward. Sunlight streaming through the gap heightens the contrast between the cedar joists and decking on the underside of the roof and the supporting beams and columns of brushed steel, which appear luminous thanks to the daylight. [Fig. 5] The dialogue between natural elements and those of human manufacture is embodied in the supplementary system of steel struts and cables, which suggests analogies with delicate vine tendrils. Sunlight piercing the vine-covered trellises that front the pavilion casts dappled green shadows on bluestone paving. Metal roofs amplify the sound of falling rain, and an extension of the copper gutter system operates as a scupper, so the sight and sound of the rainwater plunging to a storage basin below makes its potential use as nourishment for the garden palpable. The interweaving of contrasting materials and forms—natural stone walls and smoother paving stones, leafy vines and delicate steel trellises, heavy timber roof and luminous structure—is enhanced by ever-changing light conditions and the seasonal flux of planting beds.

Figures 3 & 4 (opposite) Reed Hilderbrand, Leventritt Garden, Arnold Arboretum, pedestrian approach; site plan

Figure 5 Leventritt Garden Pavilion, roof detail

Visitor Center, Polly Hill Arboretum, West Tisbury, MA (1999–2001)

Roughly coeval with the Leventritt Garden Pavilion is the Visitor Center for the Polly Hill Arboretum on Martha's Vineyard, which Thompson began during her partnership with Charles Rose. [Fig. 6] The design would provide guiding architectural principles for the independent practice that she founded while the project was being

Figure 6 Visitor Center, Polly Hill Arboretum, West Tisbury, view to entry

completed. Primary among these is a propensity to conceive of the building as deferential to its locale, in which the building organization derives from the specific attributes of the site, including its topography, its orientation to the daily path of the sun and the prevailing winds, and opportunities for vistas. Related to this is a respect for passive design principles directed to energy conservation, the roots of which can be traced to local vernacular building traditions. These include operable windows to facilitate cross ventilation; sectional variation to introduce natural light into the depth of the building; clerestory windows to amplify natural ventilation through the stack effect; and scuppers to direct rainwater from the roof to basins at grade, thereby drawing attention to its potential as nourishment for the garden. The effects of these formal gestures extend beyond practicality, yielding spaces that foster respect for the natural environs by inspiring contemplation and awe in face of the powers of nature.

The Polly Hill Arboretum, a horticultural center devoted to the study and cultivation of plants and to preservation of the historic character of the site's extensive farm and woodland, was developed by horticulturist Polly Hill (1907–2007), whose family had acquired the property in 1926 for use as a summer retreat.[1] The forty-acre tract has a distinguished history. It was one of sixteen original "home lots" created on land that Henry Luce purchased in 1669 from Sachem Josias of Takemmy (now Tisbury), chief of one of the island's Wampanoag tribes.[2] The land was farmed by Luce and his descendants, the last of whom operated a tavern on the site until 1856, and it was subsequently developed as a sheep farm. In 1957, when Hill inherited the property and took over its management, she began to test the potential for cultivating this "horticulturally impoverished" region by planting a small nursery bed from seed.[3] This painstaking process ultimately led her to challenge the limits of conventional hardiness zones by propagating her entire collection of trees and shrubs from seeds obtained from around the world. Hill studied horticulture at Longwood Gardens, Winterthur, and the University of Delaware during the postwar period, and she eventually brought twenty acres of the historic farm under cultivation while preserving forty adjoining acres as native woodland. She kept meticulous records of the process by which she introduced more than two thousand plants along the edges of the tract's open meadows while retaining the traces of its evolution from a colonial farm to a summer retreat and an arboretum.

Established in 1998 as a not-for-profit institution, the Polly Hill Arboretum is a rare example of a surviving agricultural landscape in the region. The Visitor Center was commissioned to mark the organization's transition to a public amenity.[4] In accordance with landscape architect Michael Van Valkenburgh's master plan for the Arboretum, the Visitor Center is sited immediately within the northern boundary of the original forty-acre tract—marked by a natural stone wall created as part of a sheep enclosure—so as not to impinge on its historic character. Van Valkenburgh delicately inserted a parking lot amid the woodland on the adjoining parcel to the north, and Thompson continued to draw on his expertise as she developed the design.

Thompson and Van Valkenburgh worked directly with Hill and with the project's primary benefactor David H. Smith (1932–99),

1 Polly Hill was born Mary Louisa Butcher in 1907 to Margaret and Howard Butcher, Jr.; her father was a member of the Philadelphia Stock Exchange. In 1934, she married Julian Hill (1904–96), a research chemist with DuPont who helped develop nylon.

2 pollyhillarboretum.org/about/history/ accessed April 8, 2021.

3 "About Us: Who Was Polly Hill?" pollyhillarboretum.org, accessed April 8, 2021.

4 In 2002, the corporation purchased ten additional acres to the south of the original plot of land, where a greenhouse and a nursery were created for further experimentation in 2007.

Figure 7 Visitor Center, Polly Hill Arboretum, south-facing terrace

Figure 8 Visitor Center, Polly Hill Arboretum, interior

a medical researcher and conservationist who arranged for the Vineyard Conservation Society to purchase the property. Smith established a nonprofit corporation, The Polly Hill Arboretum, Inc., to further Hill's ideals of horticultural research, education, and conservation. Hill considered the building site—amid a stand of holly and stewartia trees—to be sacred, and she sought a design that would highlight her understanding of these specimens as living beings and of the grove as a potent life force. She admired the site sensitivity of Thompson and Rose's Leeper Studio Complex at the Atlantic Center for the Arts (New Smyrna Beach, 1989–97), and she sought a related challenge to the aesthetic qualities associated with vernacular approaches to design. [See Figs. 70, 135–136]

Thompson's project consists of two small pavilions: a Visitor Center, which serves as the entrance to the Arboretum, and a service building with public restrooms. They are paired around a space to the south, which Hill referred to as the Holly Grove, where a vine-covered trellis linking the two structures shades a terrace paved in irregular bluestone. [Fig. 7] The pair of structures were constructed using a shallow foundation technique developed in Scandinavia that insulates against frost with minimal disturbance to the tree roots. Both combine the heavy timber construction evocative of regional barns with shingle cladding associated with local vernacular buildings. Their shed roofs are pitched in opposite directions, yielding contrasts in the qualities of natural light admitted to the interiors, which draws attention to the subtle differences in their material treatment.

As a single volume of just over seven hundred fifty square feet, the Visitor Center reflects Thompson's notion of the threshold as a liminal space, capable of operating in vertical as well as horizontal directions and at a range of scales to link ground and sky, building and landscape. [See Fig. 8] Its qualities as a vertical threshold derive from her fascination with the ways in which architecture might draw upon the different qualities of sunlight: as it is experienced directly overhead in the open fields or the dappled light encountered in a wooded grove, versus that which enters the sides of a building through its fenestration. Inspired by the mysterious quality of light that emanates from the oversized north-facing window in Edward Hopper's studio in Truro on Cape Cod, Thompson raised a segment of the roof to create a north-facing skylight just inside the entry. A glazed projection at the northwestern corner of the room is fitted with a bench, enabling visitors to immerse themselves in the dappled sunlight that pierces the tree canopy during the late afternoon. [See Fig. 108] The awning windows in each facade, together with banks of clerestory windows directly under the sloping roof plane, yield lighting effects that are amplified by the taller south-facing clerestory windows, which direct the visitor's glance skyward.

The dominance of windows in the entry facade and those along the south-facing terrace imparts a sense of the interior volume as an expanded threshold between the parking lot and the arboretum. [See Fig. 1] This impression was originally amplified in the vicinity of the southern facade, where the maple flooring gave way to a wedge of bluestone paving that was level with the terrace, diminishing the sense of a literal threshold between indoors and out. The continuity of interior and exterior was augmented when the maple flooring was subsequently replaced by bluestone paving throughout. During occasional summer showers, when the awning windows are left open, the room is permeated by the sound of raindrops gently falling on the roof. This experience is reiterated on the terrace, where large stone slabs salvaged from the foundations of the renovated Luce Homestead are positioned under roof overhangs, enticing visitors to linger and take in the sights and sounds of the rainwater as it plunges to a pair of stone basins below the scuppers that project from the gutters. [Fig. 9] (A lack of water in the basins would signal a potential drought). Additional seating is provided on the low mortarless stone walls that bound the terrace,

Figure 9 Visitor Center, Polly Hill Arboretum, scupper and basin

Figures 10 & 11 Visitor Center, Polly Hill Arboretum, restrooms

which are capped by large flat stones, unlike the historic sheepfold enclosures, where smaller stones are placed on top.

The form of the trellis was inspired by the Bower, a shady retreat of natural black locust boughs that provide a frame for vines, which Hill created a short distance from the Visitor Center. [See Fig. 152] Thompson used similar boughs at the top of her trellis, and she supported them on columns with a distinctive profile—machined to taper at both ends—so they appear to yield to the weight of the vines. Thin wire strands that front the south-facing clerestory windows extend from the top of the trellis to the roof, providing supports for the vines to climb the full height of the building. This augments the protection from the summer sun afforded by the roof overhangs and makes the building appear enveloped in dense summer foliage.

Thompson similarly capitalized upon the varied quality of light emitted through the restroom windows. [Figs. 10 & 11] The dappled sunlight that breaks through the tree canopy, which is visible through the tall north-facing clerestory windows, contrasts with the more enigmatic light that penetrates the frosted glass windows below. The resulting sense of the service building as a threshold between ground and sky is enhanced by its material details: the narrow slots between the cedar slats of the toilet stalls that impart an ephemeral quality of airiness to the restrooms; the thin, tapered steel supports that make the stalls appear to hover above the bluestone paving on the floor; and the related effect of the row of sinks set in a heavy slate countertop that is cantilevered from the tongue-in-groove cedar walls.

Smith associated his motivation to preserve the Polly Hill Arboretum as a public amenity with his admiration for the scientific rigor of Hill's painstaking efforts to challenge accepted horticultural norms and develop new species, which he termed "genetic engineering."[5] Her quest also engaged the spiritual as well as the historic value of the site, reflecting what one might learn from prolonged intervention in the mysteries of the natural world. Owing to its agricultural and scientific value, the property was listed on the National Register of Historic Places in 2015.

Walden Pond Visitor Center, Concord, MA (2011–16)

The reciprocity of architecture and the natural environs at the Polly Hill Arboretum is echoed in MTA's Walden Pond Visitor Center, created a decade and a half later and situated on another property of historic significance—the Walden Pond State Reservation in Concord, which had been designated a National Historic Landmark in 1962. [Fig. 12] Thompson's building occupies the northernmost segment of the extensive plot of land owned by Ralph Waldo Emerson, where Henry David Thoreau (1817–62) spent over two years of his life in the small cabin he built in the vicinity of the pond. Thompson's understanding of Thoreau's work and his respect for the spiritual dimensions of the natural world contributed to differences as well as similarities between the two MTA projects. Their most prominent points of divergence derive from her efforts in Concord to address the increased cognizance of the environmental degradation that has resulted from the human exploitation of natural resources.

To fulfill the complex requirements associated with a major tourist site, the

5 David Smith, cited by Julia Wells, "David Smith and Polly Hill Form Unusual Conservation Alliance," *The Vineyard Gazette* (5 August 1997), https://vineyardgazette.com/news/1997/08/05/david-smith-and-polly-hill-form-unusual-conservation-alliance. accessed April 10, 2021.

Figure 12 Walden Pond Visitor Center, Concord

Figure 13 Walden Pond Visitor Center, lobby/exhibition space with view to conference/screening room

Walden Pond Visitor Center includes a lobby housing a permanent exhibition, a temporary exhibition space that is used for conferences, film screenings and lectures, a bookstore, and staff offices. [Fig. 13] A trellis of black locust boughs edges the large wooden deck in front, which affords independent access to the restrooms. Although the building's heavy timber construction, locust bough trellis, and overhanging roof suggest parallels with the Visitor Center at the Polly Hill Arboretum, Thompson's approach to the Concord site differs radically from that of the earlier example.

Reflecting the increased interest in Thoreau's environmental legacy during the early twentieth century, the Walden Pond Visitor Center was the first step toward realizing the 2012 Master Plan for the Reservation, on which Thompson collaborated with the landscape architecture, planning, and urban design firm Crosbie Schlessinger Smallbridge of Boston. The planners envisioned the Visitor Center as a gateway that would open directly to the pond and its popular swimming area. Thompson convinced the planning team and representatives of the Massachusetts Department of Conservation and Recreation, who commissioned the project, that the experience of the building should be secondary to that of the pond and its wooded environs. She accordingly sited the Visitor Center across route 126, in the vicinity of an earlier administration building, the extant foundations and basement of which Thompson incorporated in her design.

Thompson engaged her frequent collaborator Van Valkenburgh Associates (MVVA) to rework and expand an existing parking lot so that automobiles would enter the parking areas from the northeast, providing them with direct southwestern views

Figure 14 Walden Pond Visitor Center, approach ramp

to the pond. She deliberately positioned her building to one side, opposite an existing replica of Thoreau's cabin.[6] [See Fig. 80] The space between these structures forms a verdant threshold to the pond, which Van Valkenburgh planted with native trees and shrubs and furnished with benches so that visitors might linger to enjoy the view. In acknowledgment of the different motivations of those who come to enjoy the Reservation's recreational amenities versus those with greater interest in its historical legacy, parking for tourist buses is accommodated east of the building, where the bookstore, exhibition spaces, and toilet facilities are accessed directly from the deck.

Thompson associates the extensive use of wood at both the Polly Hill Arboretum and Walden Pond with a sense of bodily comfort that derives from its low thermal conductivity in relation to that of metal, stone, or glass. She attributes a related effect of well-being to the visibility of the structural systems afforded by their heavy timber construction. The more complex spatial layout at Walden Pond led Thompson to maintain the visibility of the structural system by using low wooden partitions to subdivide the public spaces. [Fig. 13] The beams above fan out radially like the ribs of an umbrella, augmenting the sense of protection provided by the overhanging eaves.

In keeping with the environmental values associated with Thoreau's legacy and endorsed by the Massachusetts Department of Recreation and Conservation, Thompson sought to limit the project's ecological footprint. In contrast to the

6 Thoreau built his cabin close to the water, but it fell into ruin shortly after he left Walden Pond. After the hearth stone was discovered in 1945, a trail was created to the site.

Visitor Center for the Polly Hill Arboretum, which is firmly anchored in its site, the Walden Pond facility seems to float atop its wooden deck of heat-treated ash, which is accessed by stairs and a long ramp of the same material. [Fig. 14] This relative sense of lightness is amplified by the slim steel posts that support the locust boughs of the trellis and part of the roof overhang, in contrast to the tapered wooden columns at the Polly Hill Arboretum. [See Figs. 71 & 72] Apart from the structural beams of Douglas fir, the wood used in the construction of the Walden Pond Visitor Center originated from Massachusetts forests. Trees cut down during construction were salvaged and used to create the interior furniture and fittings. The wood siding and decking was heat-treated as a preservative, giving the building exterior the suggestive aroma of a campfire. In a more extreme example of repurposing materials, Van Valkenburgh's outdoor benches were milled from live oak timbers that had been imported from Saint Simons Island, Georgia during the 1600s and preserved in underwater storage tanks at the Charlestown Navy Yard for use in repairing the USS Constitution and other frigates. The density of live oak makes it particularly durable for outdoor use.

Like the Visitor Center at the Polly Hill Arboretum, the Walden Pond facility makes use of overhanging eaves to limit exposure to the summer sun while admitting the heat of the low-lying winter sun. Operable windows high on the facades facilitate cross ventilation, which is amplified by ceiling fans, precluding the need for air conditioning in the public zone. In Concord, moreover, Thompson augmented these passive means of energy conservation with a rooftop solar hot water system and a photovoltaic array in the northernmost parking lot that is elevated to provide shade for the cars. [See Fig. 130] The building's triple-glazed windows, LED lighting, and super-insulated walls and roof also help to limit its power requirements, so that sufficient energy is generated by the solar systems to fill the needs of both this building and the bathhouse that MTA is currently designing next to the pond.

Thoreau's stay at Walden Pond was motivated by his interest in the sights and sounds of the natural world and what they might tell us about human habitation and progress. In *Walden* (1854), he elaborated on what might be gained from such prolonged immersion in the natural environs, "I went to the woods because I wished to live deliberately, to front only the essential facts of life, and see if I could not learn what it had to teach, and not, when I came to die, discover that I had not lived."[7] While MTA's Visitor Center provides an introduction to Thoreau's philosophical outlook, it also reflects the value of impinging lightly on the site and enabling the visitor to engage directly with the ephemeral spiritual qualities of the Walden Pond State Reservation.

7 Henry David Thoreau, *Walden, or Life in the Woods* (Boston, Ticknor and Fields, 1854).

Corktown Common Park Pavilion, Toronto, Ontario, Canada (2006–11)

MTA's pavilion for Toronto's Corktown Common Park resulted from another collaboration with MVVA during the period when the Walden Pond Visitor Center was underway. Occupying a former rail yard on the banks of the Don River and adjacent to the urban core, the eighteen-acre park was to be the centerpiece of a new residential area for the city. A critical piece of flood mitigation infrastructure, the park consists of two distinct zones: a riverside prairie designed to accept floodwater and a massive landform, which Van Valkenburgh devised to shield much of downtown Toronto from potential flooding. He conceived of the undulating terrain of the landform as a simulacrum of Ontario's native landscape. A central lawn separates two distinct areas: a hill containing MTA's pavilion, which is positioned amid a rocky outcrop and associated recreational amenities, and a lower-lying aspen grove and marsh. A bicycle path that threads through the park doubles as the access route for service vehicles.

The pavilion is sited at the crest of the hill, where it serves as an orientation device within the park. It operates at two differ-

Figure 15 Corktown Common Pavilion, Toronto

ent scales. A simple one-story, shed-roofed service building houses public restrooms, a ranger's office, and a kitchenette for public use. Its self-supporting wood frame structure contrasts with the bundled steel columns that support a pair of folded roof planes. These soar overhead, signaling the pavilion's presence from afar. [Fig. 15] The distinctive roof forms relate directly to the adjoining recreational areas designed by Van Valkenburgh. The shorter roof adjoins a zone of shallow pools and bubbling fountains for water play. The taller one shelters a long concrete banquet table and opens to a playground and sledding hill. [Fig. 16] Mediating between these two roofs is a massive, concrete block hearth that heats a gathering space and warming area, which can be enclosed by retractable partitions of translucent glass, insuring year-round use of the park. A photovoltaic array on the southern face of its chimney provides electricity to supply the lighting throughout the grounds. In further support of the park's role as a vital element of urban infrastructure, runoff from the roofs and water play area are diverted to the marsh, which filters the water so that it can be used for irrigation. The large boulders that Van Valkenburgh dispersed about the pavilion's edges provide seating for adult supervision of the play areas while evoking a more remote aspect of the Canadian terrain.

Slough Farm Foundation, Edgartown, Martha's Vineyard, MA (2015–18)

A further example of Thompson's approach to the relationship between architecture and the natural environs arose with the commission to design a new educational farm and community gathering place on a forty-acre site near Slough Cove in Edgartown, Martha's Vineyard. Thompson's proclivity for creating sustainable design solutions resonated with the values of her client, the nonprofit Slough Farm Foundation. Formed in 2016, the organization promotes a regenerative, ecosystems approach to growing a biodiverse, rotating

Figure 16 Corktown Common Pavilion, concrete banquet table, bundled columns

Figure 17 Slough Farm Foundation, Edgartown, aerial view

assortment of crops and to raising heritage breeds of cattle, sheep, turkeys, chickens, and ducks, along with goats and bees. The foundation's public mission is exceptionally varied. It extends beyond farming education to include research into methods for improving soils, ponds and estuaries, and support for local food equity programs by creating and distributing single-serving meals and donating all food products not consumed on site. It fosters the integration of small-scale sustainable farming and the arts through multidisciplinary residency programs for artists who work in the fields and pastures and offer public workshops to the community.

Thompson enlisted MVVA to assist with the site planning and landscape design. The main structure of the compound is sited amid a collection of outbuildings—a cow barn, an equipment barn, a greenhouse, and a silo. It contains a yoga/music studio, a Great Room with a demonstration kitchen for community events, living quarters for the farmer and for participants in the residency program, small animal quarters, and related service spaces. **[Fig. 17]** The building is segmented into public areas and farm functions. Linkages among its various zones and external farm components were important for the project's intended symbolism as well as for the day-to-day operations of the foundation. For example, the Great Room—a gathering space situated between the bedrooms for participants in the residency program and the wing for small farm animals—is a variation on the traditional farm house kitchen. **[Fig. 19]** There, local chefs demonstrate inventive ways to use the farm produce. Its windows open to a small paddock, which enables the goats, alpacas, and sheep to peer into the activities taking place in the space. **[Fig. 18]** A service stair concealed in the pantry leads to a basement-level commercial kitchen, where local chefs prepare meals for the food donation program. Produce is stored in an adjoining root cellar, while a rustic stone stairway designed by Van Valkenburgh leads from the basement kitchen up to the greenhouse and the vegetable garden.

The functional relationships among the parts of the program inspired Thompson to adapt the traditional form of the New

England connected farmstead—in which residence and farm buildings are attached in a linear organization—to create a pair of open courtyards. The larger courtyard is associated with the public functions of the foundation and the smaller one with its farm functions. This layout derives from that of the earlier structures on the site, which were in a poor state of repair, necessitating their demolition. By building on the footprint of the former farm structures, Thompson not only facilitated the approval process for creating a new educational facility in an area zoned for residential use but also drew upon the social potential of the courtyard form. In support of the foundation's communal aspirations, the large, pea-gravel courtyard is used to host farmers' markets, film screenings, dance parties, and outdoor yoga classes, among other events. Van Valkenburgh fitted it with large granite slabs and inserted a copse of trees to form a sitting area for smaller group activities.

Shingled facades, tall double-hung windows, a cedar shake roof, and a heavy timber structure evoke the aesthetic qualities of a traditional farmhouse. These allusions to the conventional farmstead are reinforced by the distinctive massing that derives from the juxtaposition of the building's programmatic components. At the center of the layout is the Great Room, which is linked in one direction to the visiting residents' quarters and a yoga/music studio and in the other direction to small animal stalls and the farmer's residence. Rather than circumscribing the activities taking place within them, these segments comprise spaces in which a range of foundation activities might occur. An open quality prevails in the courtyard, where large, wood-framed sliding glass doors lead directly to the yoga/music studio and Great Room. To signify the foundation's public essence, these oversized doors evoke the sliding barn doors that provide access to the animal stalls.

Aspects of the building layout derive from the position of the silo, which was the only element of the earlier farm structures that was retained.[8] The decision to restore the silo was made for symbolic rather than pragmatic reasons, as it is no longer used to store feed for the animals. Locally, it aligns with the Great Room, reflecting the importance of the farm operations to the foundation's public programs. Rising above the environs' sandplain grasslands, moreover, the silo operates as a beacon, signaling the presence of the Slough Farm Foundation from afar. Its potential to ultimately house an observatory holds the promise of broader cosmological connections.

8 Known as "widow makers" for their propensity to collapse when not property maintained, concrete stave silos utilize galvanized steel hoops to compress the walls, which are protected by a cementitious coating. A Mennonite family from Pennsylvania was enlisted to carry out the renovation, which involved adding an inner layer of concrete, six inches thick, to ensure the silo's structural integrity.

Figures 18 & 19 Slough Farm Foundation: window to paddock; Great Room

Elsewhere on the property a new cow barn was created on the site of an earlier structure, the metal frame of a corn crib was planted with vines to form a shady retreat, and the flower garden was revived in its original location, where it adjoins a new vegetable garden and greenhouse. [See Figs. 133 & 161] An equipment barn and guest house were added on an adjoining property. In keeping with the foundation's environmental ethos, the compound features heavy timber construction of reclaimed white oak and an extensive gray water system. Rainwater from the roofs is stored underground in rain hogs for use in irrigating the grounds, while a rooftop photovoltaic array aids in alleviating the farm's energy needs.

Figure 20 Charlesbank Landing Pavilion, perspective from the Charles River

Charlesbank Landing Pavilion, Charles River Esplanade, Boston, MA (2017–18, 2023–)

As the first new construction on Boston's Charles River Esplanade in over fifty years, MTA's Charlesbank Landing Pavilion is part of a larger effort to revitalize a segment of the Charles River landscape that had fallen into disuse over the previous decades. The The Massachusetts Department of Conservation and Recreation and The Explanade Association commissioned Thompson to design this new facility following the success of her Walden Pond Visitor Center. The pavilion will serve as a visitor center and exhibition space, while housing support spaces for the Esplanade's recreational venues. It will be built in two stages on a plot of land near the eastern end of the Esplanade that dates from the Charlesbank expansion of 1947–49, which was previously occupied by the Lee Pool (1951).[9] The first stage includes an exhibition space, a café, and public restrooms surmounted by Esplanade Association offices, an adjoining soccer field, and a storage yard for the Department of Conservation and Recreation. In the second phase, the soccer field will be converted into a multipurpose sports hall, which, with the addition of a catering kitchen, will accommodate large community events. Despite its straightforward program and modest form, the Charlesbank Landing Pavilion serves a larger symbolic purpose: introducing visitors and residents to the Esplanade's recreational amenities and linking them indirectly to the Emerald Necklace—the 1,100-acre linear chain of parks designed by Frederick Law Olmsted that connects the Boston Common and Public Garden to the Back Bay Fens, the Arboretum, and Franklin Park.

Lying between the Charlesbank Playground and the Red Sox Teddy Ebersol's Baseball Fields, the site occupies an extension to Frederick Law Olmsted's Charlesbank proposal of 1892, which was intended to serve the lower income population of the West End. It included the first open-air public gymnasia in the United States to be operated free of charge, with separate facilities for men and women, and early examples of "sand courts" (sandboxes) for children, all supervised by trained instructors.[10] After 1910, when construction of the Charles River Dam transformed the tidal marshes and mud flats of the Charles River into a fresh water river basin and riverfront park, Charlesbank was incorporated into the Esplanade in accordance with Arthur Shurcliff's designs of 1928–36 as well as his further improvements following the creation of Storrow Drive (beginning in 1949), which severed direct pedestrian access from the West End.

9 The Lee Pool (1951) was closed as irreparable in the 1990s and demolished in 2019.

10 For the history of the Charlesbank extension of the Esplanade, see Nancy S. Seasholes, *Gaining Ground: A History of Landmaking in Boston* (Cambridge and London: MIT Press, 2003), 122–32.

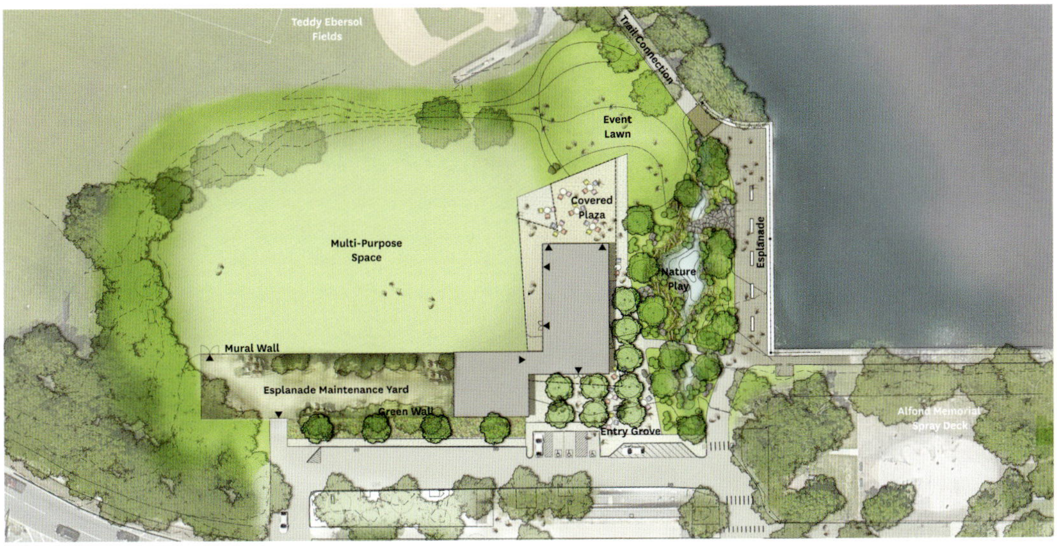

Figure 21 MVVA, Charlesbank Landing Pavilion, site plan

This history of the Charlesbank segment of the Esplanade as a public recreational venue will be featured in the lobby/exhibition space of Thompson's pavilion. The roof terrace, accessed by a long ramp leading up from the riverfront, will serve as a viewing platform for soccer games and for sailing events on the Charles River. **[Fig. 20]** MVVA's proposal for the Charlesbank Landing landscape will broaden the programmatic aspect of the pavilion by including an entry grove, a pollinator garden, a rain garden for stormwater retention, a zone for nature education, a riverfront classroom with tiered, natural seating, and an event lawn **[Fig. 21]**.

◆ ◆ ◆

MTA's park pavilions, visitors centers, and educational and recreational venues reflect diverse relationships to their locales: as thresholds to the experience of the broader site at the Polly Hill Arboretum, the Charles River Esplanade, and Slough Farm; as ancillary to the landscape of the Boston Arboretum and the Walden Pond State Reservation; and as a destination in Toronto's Corktown Common Park. They also reflect different ways of serving the public: advancing the educational missions of the Polly Hill Arboretum (horticulture), the Slough Farm Foundation (sustainable agriculture and animal husbandry) and the Boston Esplanade Association (history of the locale); furthering the research agendas of the Arnold Arboretum, the Polly Hill Arboretum, and the Slough Farm Foundation; and supporting recreational opportunities at Corktown Common Park and Charlesbank Landing. Whether by providing an antidote to the environmental degradation that resulted from Toronto's industrial past or by drawing upon the conservation ethos in Concord, the farming tradition on Martha's Vineyard, or the sequence of public open spaces in Boston, the buildings in each case serve to reinforce the interrelationship of architecture and the natural realm.

Figure 22 Overleaf Corktown Common Pavilion, Toronto.

Architecture as Communal Experience

Throughout her practice, Maryann Thompson responds to the programmatic challenges invoked by her commissions to promote human interaction at a range of scales and in a variety of settings. She accomplishes this objective through various architectural means, by introducing protracted entry sequences and novel programmatic elements, for example, or by establishing distinctive relationships with the broader community or the natural environs. This particular attribute of her work derives from the extensive participation of clients, community groups, and other interested parties in the design process.

The three examples cited in this chapter, which are roughly contemporaneous, reflect diverse scales and settings in which such interaction was of particular relevance. At the Eli and Edythe L. Broad Institute in Cambridge, the focus was on fostering communication among scientists from diverse disciplines. At the Temple Ahavat Achim in Gloucester, the purpose was not only to cultivate interrelationships among the congregants but also to affirm their substantive connections with the historic seaside community. With the Jonathan Milikowsky Science and Technology Center for The Foote School in New Haven, the programmatic requirements encompassed spaces for collaboration and socialization in the broader campus environment as well as in the building. In each case, Thompson sought to encourage opportunities for gathering and impromptu encounters by creating spaces of solitude or contemplation.

Eli and Edythe L. Broad Institute, Cambridge, MA (2004–06)

Emblematic of this phenomenon is the Eli and Edythe L. Broad Institute, an innovative Harvard-MIT collaborative research environment co-founded in 2004 by Eric Lander, professor of systems biology at MIT and director of the White House Office of Science and Technology Policy under President Joseph Biden. [Fig. 23]

Lander conceived of the Institute as a means to overcome the hermeticism frequently associated with scientific research. His concept of a "commons" for the scientific community, in which research results would be open and broadly accessible, arose following the sequencing of the Human Genome Project—an international effort in which he played a significant leadership role. Lander envisioned the Institute as a means to amplify understanding of the genetic basis of disease and to foster prevention, diagnosis, and treatment. Dedicated to

Figure 23 Eli and Edythe L. Broad Institute, Cambridge

creative risk-taking, it combines research in biology, chemistry, mathematics, computation, and engineering with medical science and clinical research at a scale normally seen in industry. In response to this challenge, Thompson sought architectural means to foster interdisciplinary discourse and the cross-fertilization of ideas by optimizing opportunities for impromptu encounters and interactions among the Institute faculty and their associates from the region's affiliated educational institutions and medical schools.

Such interaction is promoted primarily through three architectural means: a protracted entry sequence, orchestrated to bring scientists from different laboratories into contact with each other and with the public; the introduction of novel programmatic elements amidst the office and laboratory spaces as potential sites of spontaneous encounter; and a reliance on physical transparency throughout the building, in accordance with Lander's vision of an open and transparent scientific process.

A bank of glass doors along the street front renders the activities in the generous ground floor entrance hall. These are used to provide access to large group events in the lobby and its adjoining auditorium. Those entering individually or in small clusters, either to peruse the ground-floor exhibitions or to work in the building, pass through an adjacent glazed vestibule, where admittance is monitored. Seating provided for groups of various sizes has made the double-height lobby a hub of activity, where scientists and their associates from the various laboratories can mingle with the occasional visitors

Figure 24 Eli and Edythe L. Broad Institute, lobby viewed from mezzanine

or confer on their work in progress before continuing to the bank of elevators, deliberately placed toward the rear of the volume, beyond a second security point. [Fig. 24]

Each of the six laboratory floors features a lobby with furniture arranged in a living room-like setting. This adjoins an open kitchen/bar and a conference room that can be closed off by a vitreous accordian wall. [Fig. 25] Each floor is subdivided into discrete zones of offices and laboratory spaces that are separated by double glass doors. Although these work spaces are enclosed by glazed partitions to assure visibility of the work in progress, certain laboratories also open directly to the corridor, fulfilling Lander's concept of a "sock path" to encourage the scientists and technicians to mingle informally among themselves. [Figs. 26 & 27] Others are cordoned off to maintain hygienic work environments. The glazed facades that wrap the volume of laboratories on four of the building's seven upper levels not only provide light-filled work spaces for the scientists but also encourage public awareness of the research undertaken at the Institute, rendering Lander's concept of a transparent work environment visible from the public domain.

Figures 25–27 Eli and Edyth I. Broad Institute: kitchen/bar and setting area; glass enclosed offices; typical laboratory floor plan (with sock path indicated in yellow)

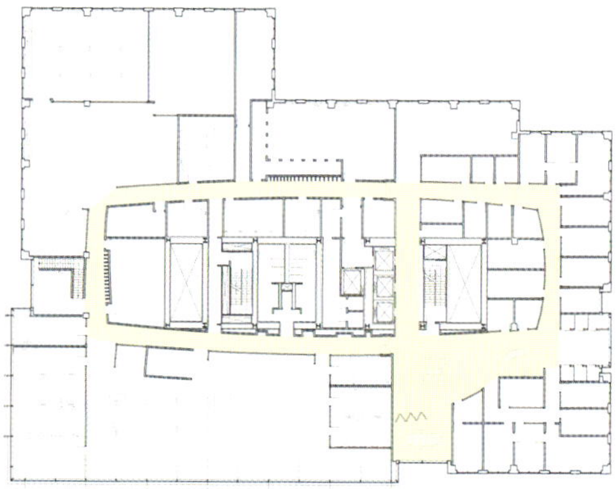

Figure 28 Temple Ahavat Achim, Gloucester

Temple Ahavat Achim, Gloucester, MA (2009–12)

The commission to design the Temple Ahavat Achim in the heart of the seaport town of Gloucester posed a distinct set of challenges concerning not only the internal needs of this religious community but also its integral relationship with the town's historic center. The Temple is both a site of religious worship and a community center, a place for members to gather throughout the week, where classes in yoga and dance are offered along with those in Hebrew and the Torah. The project provided MTA the possibility to address the specific needs of this orthodox Jewish group of some two hundred families in ways that its earlier structure, a former church building converted to a synagogue that was tragically destroyed by fire, could not.[1]

A protracted entry sequence offers an opportunity for congregants to pause and reflect on their institution's relationship with its historic context and the natural conditions of its environs as well as on internal relationships among the community of worshippers. Thompson devised the building's deep, layered threshold to shield congregants from the harsh winter winds that arise from the north while enhancing access to the cooling summer breezes that emanate from the west. [Fig. 28] Set within a smooth stone wall of the outer facade is a heavy wooden door—the lone survivor of the fire that destroyed the original building and a symbol of the congregation's ongoing presence in the community. It leads not to the building interior but to an outdoor passageway—a covered terrace—that extends the full length of the structure. Pierced openings in the eastern end of the facade modulate the sunlight that streams into this passage, imparting a sense of mystery and wonder. [Fig. 29] A second door overlooking the adjoining garden provides access to the interior. This is followed by a line of benches, also facing the garden, that offers congregation members an area for quiet contemplation prior to entry—a space where they are alternately warmed by the low-lying winter sun or protected from its harsh summer glare. [Fig. 30] The seating overlooks a random pattern of paving stones set in the lawn, which are positioned beneath a scupper to disperse the rainfall during

1 In 1950, Temple Ahavat Achim purchased the former church building on its central Gloucester site and converted it into a synagogue; the structure was destroyed by fire in 2007.

inclement weather, marking a relationship between ground and sky.

An issue for the internal layout was how to convey a sense of community in a structure capable of accommodating a limited number of participants for the regular weekly services and events along with larger groups of worshippers during the High Holy days. This was accomplished by providing amenities for ongoing weekly activities on the ground floor, together with a large flexible space on the floor above that is used intermittently, both as a sanctuary and as a social hall for special occasions.

The congregation refers to the segmented ground floor lobby as the "schmoozatorium." It consists of an open sequence of volumes that are distinct in character and devised to accommodate a range of uses and types of accommodation. Apart from its seating areas of diverse sizes, the lobby has a library-like space fitted with bookshelves and a long table for studying that overlooks the garden. [Figs. 31 + 32] This zone leads to a set of small meeting rooms, where occasional classes are held. Secluded in the northeastern corner is the Beit Midrash, which accommodates up to sixty worshippers and

Figures 29 & 30
Temple Ahavat Achim: lighting effects in layered facade; external entry passage

Figures 31 & 32
Temple Ahavat Achim: ground floor plan; lobby study area

doubles as a study space, with bookshelves and tables lining its walls. The private nature of the Beit Midrash, with its controlled means of access, contrasts with the openness of the lobby, where a mixture of uses throughout the week imparts the sense of a vibrant social atmosphere that is evident to passersby and members alike.

Visible from the entry is a broad staircase at the back of the lobby. Lit by clerestory windows that accentuate the duality of earth and sky, it leads to the foyer to the large hall on the floor above. Folding wooden screens enable the volume of the hall to be subdivided to accommodate different uses: a large sanctuary with a capacity for three hundred worshippers; a smaller sanctuary for one hundred eighty-five together with a social hall that can hold sixty-five individuals seated at tables and is serviced by an adjoining kitchen; or an expanded social hall that can accommodate large groups for dance or yoga classes or up to two hundred diners seated at tables [Fig. 33]. In accordance with Jewish custom, the eastern

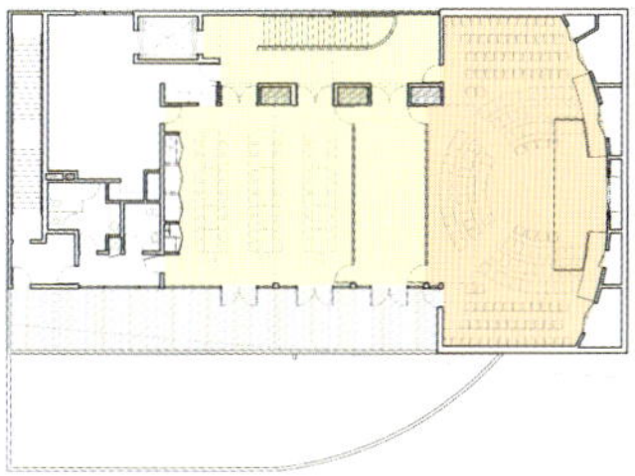

Social Hall: Dining space for up to 65 people; Sanctuary for up to 85 worshippers

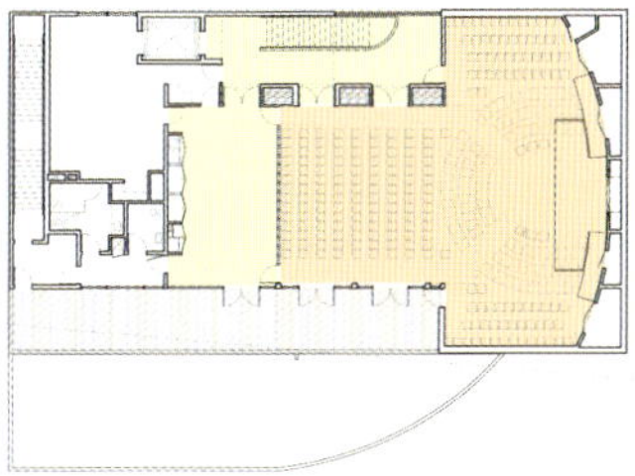

Expanded Sanctuary for up to 175 worshippers

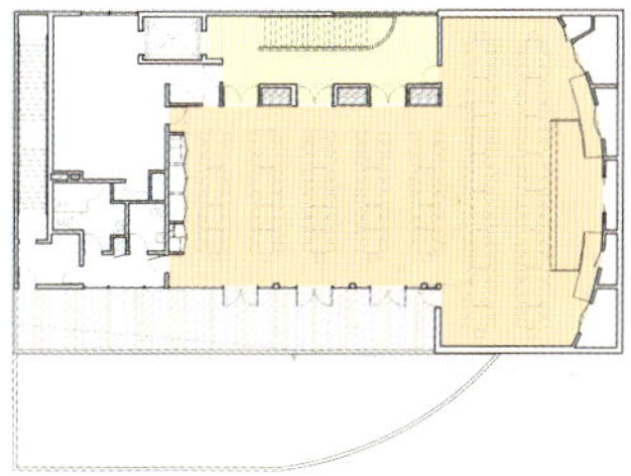

Expanded Sanctuary for up to 300 worshippers

Figures 33 & 34
Temple Ahavat Achim: upper level plan variations; Sanctuary

end of the room houses the Torah. [Fig. 34] Kept in the ark, which appears to be part of the wall, its presence is marked by ceiling fixtures that are always lit. To reorient the space in a manner appropriate to its secular uses, a white curtain can be moved along a ceiling track to conceal direct views of the cabinet, while the presence of the Torah is signified by the persistent glow of the light. During the High Holy services, when the rabbi stands on a demountable thrust stage or bimah, he faces the Torah rather than the worshippers, thereby accentuating his role as a member of the community of congregants. Clerestory windows beneath the hall's canted ceiling planes afford views to the spires of Gloucester's City Hall and a church steeple as well as occasional seagulls, reinforcing the members' sense of connection to the heart of this historic seaside community.

Jonathan Milikowsky Science and Technology Center, The Foote School, New Haven, CT (2009–12)

The opportunity to design a new Science and Technology Center for The Foote School in New Haven, Connecticut, inspired Thompson to further the sense of community among faculty and students by enhancing the building's integral relationship with its environs—both built and natural—thereby expanding upon the master plan for the eighteen-acre campus she had developed in partnership with Charles Rose. [Figs. 35 & 36] The distinctive pedagogy of this private school for grades kindergarten to ninth grade is grounded in the philosophy that "learning builds community." Students are encouraged "to ask questions and discover connections, to think and work independently, collaboratively, and creatively."[2] Moreover, outdoor learning is a significant aspect of The Foote School curriculum.

The configuration of Thompson's building reflects a response to the various scales of the problem: its connection to the broader campus; its engagement with adjoining open areas and buildings; the relationship between exterior and interior spaces; and internal programmatic requirements. At each scale, Thompson created

2 "Mission and Philosophy," www.footeschool.org, accessed 29 April 2021.

Figure 35 Jonathan Milikowski Science and Technology Center, The Foote School, New Haven, principal entrance from the Middle School Center

1. Existing Vehicular Drop Off
2. Sacred Grove
3. Campus Center
4. Administration Library
5. Arts and Music
6. Gymnasium Theater
7. Middle School Center
8. Science and Technology Center
9. New Vehicular Drop Off

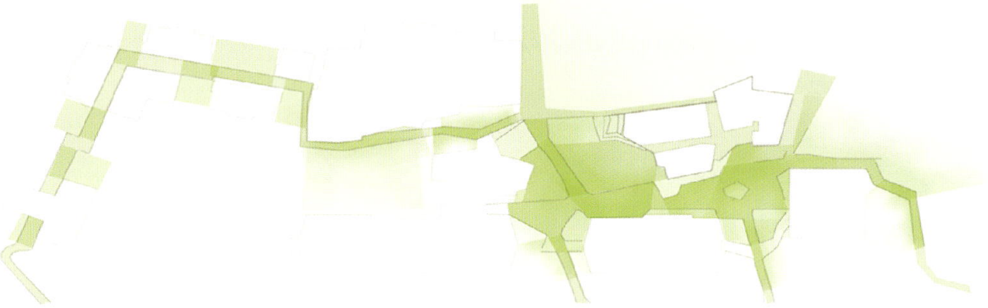

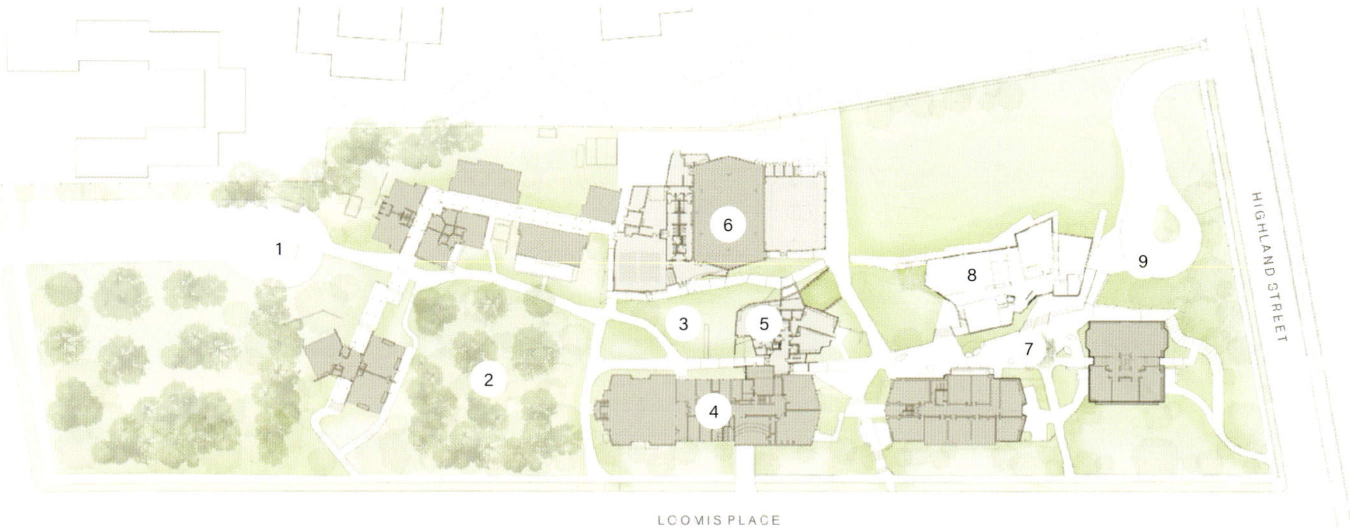

Figure 36 The Foote School: diagram of pedestrian circulation routes; site plan

spaces for impromptu and organized encounters among small groups of students and faculty as well as settings for broader community engagement.

The original campus facilities were completed in 1958 to the design of architects Carlton and Diana Allyn Granbery. In keeping with the pedagogical significance of the outdoors as a learning environment, they distributed discrete groupings of buildings along the length of the site—a narrow strip of land atop a plateau that rises above a hilly, verdant residential neighborhood. A vehicular drop off at the southern end of the property leads to a group of classroom buildings for the youngest students that are linked by covered passageways and loosely organized around a densely wooded area, known as the Sacred Grove. A combination administrative building/library and a gymnasium occupy the middle of the site; these are followed by the classroom buildings for the older children to the north, which lie opposite a sports field. Five sets of staircases that lead up to the plateau are distributed along the residential street to the east, providing independent access to the discrete segments of the campus.

In their campus plan of 1999, Thompson and Rose enhanced spatial definition of the existing sequence of open spaces through their architectural additions, which house facilities for art, music, and theater as components of the overall curriculum.

Rather than combine these elements in one creative arts building, the architects distributed them around a new communal open space, accommodating classrooms for the visual arts and music in an extension to the library/administration building and creating the theater as an annex to the gymnasium, which was enlarged as part of this building campaign. With these revisions, the open lawn of the new Campus Center became a central organizational device for the school and the staircase leading up to it the primary pedestrian entrance.

To accommodate the growing enrollment of the student body, Thompson was asked to provide a new building for eighth and ninth grades, with classrooms that reflect a curricular emphasis on science and technology in keeping with STEM initiatives to encourage student interest in those areas. She reconfigured the campus entry sequence by adding a vehicular drop-off point at the northern end of the property and linking it to the meandering pedestrian circulation route and network of open spaces. The building layout was devised to work in conjunction with two of the original middle school buildings to form a new Middle School Center, where the pedestrian path now originates. Unlike the Sacred Grove or the verdant expanse of the Campus Center, this space is shaded by a large, preexisting red oak tree, dotted with boulders, and paved in asphalt so that it can be filled with chairs and used for ceremonial purposes, such as graduation exercises. **[Fig. 35]**

The requirement that the science classrooms have direct access to outdoor teaching spaces led Thompson to give her two-story

Figure 37 Jonathan Milikowsky Science and Technology Center, view from the southwest

building the topographic character of a constructed terrain. This tactic enabled her to capitalize upon the gradual slope of the site as it rises from east to west and south to north. Thompson elevated the east side of the building on a low plinth, where the main entrance is reached by a broad set of stairs that rise from the Middle School Center as well as a shallow ramp that rises from the vehicular drop off point. At the southern end of the building, a sequence of grass-covered terraces serves as seating for outdoor assembles or informal social encounters. [Fig. 37] The ground-floor science classrooms open to a terrace along the west side of the building, while glazed, oversized garage doors in the second-floor biology and physics classrooms open fully to the large, south-facing deck that is fitted with raised planting beds and doubles as an outdoor teaching space. [Fig. 38] The network of connections between the classrooms and the campus is emphasized by a pair of external staircases that provide independent access from the deck to diverse points in the immediate environs.

Through its three-dimensional organization, the building operates as a threshold to each of its adjoining spaces, providing both visual and physical links to the campus. Along its northern face, a pair of ramps lead from the vehicular drop off up to the building entry and down to the Middle School Center. To the east, a system of stairs and benches at the entry works with the overhanging roof to create a portal to the Middle School Center. A covered deck that lines the western face of the building serves as a viewing platform for the sports field, while the stepped terraces to the south provide a direct connection between the upper-level deck and the ground plane.

Figure 38 Jonathan Milikowsky Science and Technology Center, science classroom and teaching deck

The fluid spatial sequence is echoed in the building interior. Just inside the entry, a double-height lobby affords views to the sinuous arrangement of spaces on both levels. [Fig. 39] Thompson conceived of the corridors as interior counterparts to the intimate spaces for socializing and small group meetings that proliferate throughout the campus. She gave them ample proportions and irregular layouts and lined distinct areas on each level with benches to serve as lounges for the seventh and eighth grade students respectively. She reiterated this use of seating to foster spontaneous encounters just outside the principal entry, where the ramp leading from the drop off point ends in a long wooden bench that sits above a concrete bench at the base of the plinth. This seating lines the edge of the Middle School Center, while a third bench faces the vehicular drop off point.

In keeping with its pedagogic focus, the Milikowsky Science and Technology Center is a dynamic teaching tool that reflects sustainable approaches to energy use in a manner that amplifies the interrelationships between the building and its environs. These include common-sense passive design strategies: deep roof overhangs and wooden louvers to protect the southern and western exposures; operable windows set high in the facades that work with ceiling fans to facilitate cross-ventilation through the stack effect; and a reliance on natural daylighting to reduce energy consumption. In addition, a louvered trellis that faces the playing field diffuses western sun exposure and operates as a solar thermal system to provide hot water for the building, while south-facing roofs are equipped with photovoltaic panels to supply electricity. [See Figs. 113 & 114] An interactive learning display installed in the lobby was intended to track the building's water and energy use and production, making the effects of these active and passive methods of energy conservation visible. Although this system has never been fully implemented, faculty can take advantage of the data it records in conjunction with weather data to study the potential for building in an environmentally sustainable manner.

The architectural ramifications of The Foote School's didactic emphasis on independent and collaborative inquiry are evident at every scale of Thompson's design. Students make full use of the meeting areas at the building entrance and in the hallways, the integrated classrooms and outdoor decks, and the terraces that step down to the broader campus landscape. [Fig. 40] In both its relationship to the external environs and its details, moreover, the Milikowsky Science and Technology Center embodies a broader objective: that of cultivating respect for the natural environment, thereby preparing students to become responsible citizens of the world.

◆◆◆

The use of architectural means to prompt social encounters occurs at diverse scales and in different contexts throughout Thompson's work. Although this phenomenon is particularly germane to the interiors of her school buildings, it is also characteristic of MTA's civic buildings, private residences, and outdoor settings of various types. It reflects Thompson's philosophy that, rather than circumscribing the activities that are intended to take place in a particular space, architecture should comprise spaces in which a broad range of activities might occur. As such, it is the stage on which we enact the rituals of our daily lives.

Figure 39 Jonathan Milikowsky Science and Technology Center, lobby/student lounge

Figure 40 Overleaf Jonathan Milikowsky Science and Technology Center, view from the southwest

EXIT

Architecture of Early Childhood Education

A series of commissions to design primary schools and child care centers afforded MTA opportunities to explore the architectural ramifications of contemporary approaches to early childhood education, which have long-standing roots in the theories of Swiss educational reformer Johann Heinrich Pestalozzi (1746–1827), German pedagogue Friedrich Fröbel (1782–1852), Italian physician and educator Maria Montessori (1870–1952), and Swiss psychologist Jean Piaget (1896–1980), among others. Consistent among the pedagogical principles advocated by these early theorists is the notion of directing the earliest school years to the "whole child"—to the full scope of children's individual and collective engagement with the world.

The directors of these schools and day-care centers draw particular inspiration from the Reggio Emilia approach to early childhood education, formulated by psychologist Loris Malaguzzi (1920–94) during the post-war period in Northern Italy, in which the spaces that children occupy are understood to play an active and integral role in making learning meaningful. In the Reggio Emilia classroom, the focus is not only on how the spaces look, but on how they are perceived and understood from the vantage point of the child.

In these projects, Thompson probes the potential for architecture to be an active agent in fostering the social, sensual, and emotional, as well as the cognitive capabilities of children by nurturing their inherent curiosity, creative impulses, and sense of place in relation to the natural world. Through a design philosophy predicated on embodiment, on children's sensuous engagement with materials of both human and natural origin, she conceives of each design as an invitation for the youthful occupants of these facilities to explore protracted spatial sequences by haptic, olfactory, and auditory as well as visual means, thereby expanding on Malaguzzi's educational methods to encompass a broader objective of cultivating respect for the natural environment.

Atrium School, Watertown, MA (2005–06)

Forced to vacate the property that had served as the base for its first twenty-five years in operation, the directors of the Atrium School commissioned MTA to adapt an existing warehouse to their needs. The project is intended to instill the value of resource conservation, in keeping with the objective of preparing students to be environmentally responsible citizens.

Figure 41 Atrium School, Watertown, rain garden with principal entry ramp beyond

Figure 42 Maryann Thompson, Atrium School, garden sketch, 2005

Physical restrictions imposed by the 16,000 square-foot structure, which was elevated half a level above a partially submerged basement and had limited fenestration, inspired Thompson to devise a set of formal tactics that she would continue to probe in further examples of this building type. The range of classrooms and auxiliary spaces needed to accommodate the staff and one hundred twenty children between the ages of five and twelve years led to the basic organization of classrooms distributed along a meandering, double-loaded corridor, with collective spaces—a large, open multipurpose volume and a more intimate library—at either end. In reconceptualizing these basic programmatic elements, Thompson developed the corridor as well as the classrooms and activity spaces to accommodate multiple uses.

Transforming the elevated loading dock into a covered outdoor deck, she fitted the southwestern end of the building with glazed, oversized garage doors that open directly to the large multipurpose hall—an indoor/outdoor instructional and recreational space that is used for weekly school-wide assemblies, music sessions, theatrical presentations, and gym classes. A broad ramp that rises along the northwestern edge of the hall provides access to the building. [See Fig. 111]

The only option for further outdoor play space was a parcel just beyond this end of the structure, which rises from a low point half a level below the classrooms. Working in collaboration with Michael Blier, a founding principal of Landworks Studio, Thompson conceived of the traditional school playground as a garden. It consists of three terraces—a rain garden strewn with large boulders, a small play yard, and a sweeping lawn—each with its own water collection reservoir. [Fig. 42] The lowest segment of this layered, overtly constructed landscape is nourished by rainwater runoff from the roof in a process made both visible and audible through architectural means. During a storm the rainwater is conducted to a giant scupper that extends above the end of the ramp, where it splashes dramatically over a concrete spillway before plunging through a grill that opens to a storage basin beneath the garden. A fourth terrace, paved in asphalt to fulfill the city's requirement to accommodate further parking, is used as a basketball court. The garden sequence was thus envisioned as both an integral aspect of the school's pedagogic approach and a public amenity for the neighborhood.

Rather than enter the building directly from the vehicular drop-off point, the children begin each school day by encountering the natural milieu of the rain garden before they arrive at the base of the ramp that ascends in a gradual curve to a brightly lit atrium—an extension of the multipurpose hall. [Fig. 43] As a subtly tilted ground plane, the ramp imparts the sense of a gradual transition from garden to building—an

Figure 43 Atrium School, atrium and multipurpose hall

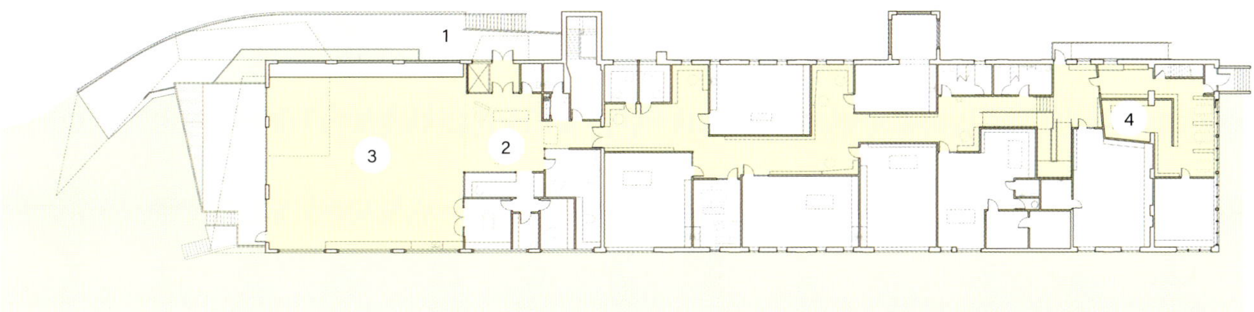

experience that differs significantly from that of the narrow stairway off the deck, which is used during the school day for more direct access to the rain garden and play yard.

The foyer leads to the offices and classrooms that are distributed in a seemingly random pattern about the meandering central corridor. [Fig. 44] Challenging the conventional role of the double-loaded corridor as the most efficient means of providing access to classrooms, Thompson distributed rooms of sizes and configurations that vary according to age of students or subject requirements along the building perimeter to yield an irregular passageway capable of playing a more substantive role in the school's educational mission. A child's sense of discovery is prompted by the intermittent presence of natural light, which is admitted at either end of the building as well as through windows that line a pair of alcoves that punctuate the sequence. [Fig. 45] Lined with benches, these alcoves serve as breakout spaces for occasional meetings, small group encounters, or quiet interludes for reading or study. Through selective use of color, the corridor walls are treated as discrete planar surfaces, which amplifies the sense of spatial layering in the passageway and its lack of a singular vanishing point.

Terminating the corridor is a wooden switchback ramp that rises half a level to the final segment of the building, which originally housed offices and was modified

Figure 44 Atrium School, plan

Figure 45 Maryann Thompson, Atrium School, sketch of reading alcove (2005)

Figure 46 Atrium School, internal ramp

to include a classroom, a language arts room, and a library. [Fig. 46] Marking a pause in the student's trajectory, the ramp is positioned at a right angle to the dominant direction of movement in the corridor. The effect of this shift in orientation is amplified by the change in flooring material that is sensed underfoot—from the concrete of the corridor to the wood of the ramp—and more palpably through direct contact with its metal handrail.

While drawing upon the industrial character of the warehouse, Thompson introduced several modifications to impart an ambiance more suited to the building's new use. On the interior, its exposed steel trusses and structural piers are painted white, and new ductwork and lighting conduits are threaded through the open webs of the trusses to enhance the children's understanding of the building systems. On the exterior, the shallow gable roof over the assembly hall is raised to admit natural light above the covered ramp. This provided an opportunity to augment the institutional appearance of the principal entry facade by covering its new triangular segment in cedar siding, which is echoed in panels beneath the windows on the side facades. At the opposite end of the building, where the school is most visible from the adjoining residential neighborhood, its identity is announced by signage mounted atop strips of western red cedar on a segment of the existing brick facade, reinforcing the sense of its vital public presence. [Fig. 47]

Measures taken to diminish the building's reliance on fossil fuels include double glazing in the windows, highly efficient mechanical and plumbing systems, and the use of recycled materials whenever feasible. To minimize the need for artificial lighting in the classrooms, new windows openings were introduced in the side facades, together with operable skylights in the roof, which provide for cross ventilation and draw out excess heat through the stack effect. Such concern for energy conservation through both active and passive means constitutes a hallmark of Thompson's design commissions.

Figure 47 Atrium School, sign

Owing to the eighteen-month eviction notice imposed by the city of Watertown, design and construction had to proceed rapidly. Weekly meetings with the school principal, chairman of the board of directors, and faculty members began in October 2005, which enabled Thompson to quickly develop the layout and obtain design approval. Construction began the following March, and the renovation was carried out in time for the school to begin operating out of its new faculty in August 2006. The success of this venture led the school to commission MTA to renovate the lower level of the building (2012–14) so the curriculum could be expanded to include the seventh and eighth grades.

The Children's School, Stamford, CT (2003–07)

A markedly different set of challenges arose in 2003, when Thompson was asked to accommodate the growth of an existing private elementary and preschool by creating a new building on its 4.4-acre wooded site that is set within a quiet residential neighborhood and includes two historic dwellings that house members of its staff. Community involvement from the outset of the commission—with faculty members, students,

1 Margaret F. Skutch and Wilfrid G. Hamlin, "Environmental Flexibility for Preschoolers," *The Phi Delta Kappan* 56, no. 5 [Special issue on the Unrecognized Environmental Curriculum] (January 1975): 326–28, here 326.

parents, and neighbors—stimulated broad investment in the project and facilitated the zoning variance needed for its construction. By redirecting automobile access via a long driveway that winds through the site, MTA was able to appease neighbors' concerns about lines of cars interfering with traffic on the residential street. [Fig. 48]

The commission was to replace a one-room Montessori School, erected on the site in 1967 by its founding director Margaret Skutch, whose educational philosophy had particular resonance with Thompson's design approach. In an effort to build upon children's inherent inquisitiveness and enhance their self-confidence, Skutch embraced a wholistic education that supports and nurtures all areas of children's development and learning. Valuing the individuality of the children in her care, she viewed the function of the teacher as guiding students to learn from each other rather than didactically imparting information, thus drawing upon their innate curiosity and problem-solving skills. Children are presented with a range of places and experiences, people, tools, and resources with which to work in a self-directed manner. Skutch sought a flexible learning environment, an open volume composed of "centers of interest ... rather than walls," conceived of as an integral part of the natural world, and capable of meeting the changing needs of her pupils.[1] Architect Ingrid Strong, who attended The Children's School as a child, brought the work of MTA to the attention

Figure 48 The Children's School, Stamford, aerial view

of the school's current director, Maureen Murphy, and collaborated in the endeavor, bringing the perspective of an insider to the school's distinct pedagogical methods.

Thompson conceived of the architecture as an active instrument in the educational process. To impart a scale appropriate to the one hundred twenty children, aged two to eight years, to be accommodated in this 15,000 square-foot building, she adapted Skutch's vision of one-room schoolhouse by subdividing the structure into two principal zones. **[Fig. 49]** The younger children, who attend for half a day, are provided for in the eastern segment of the building, with its optimum access to morning light, while the areas for the older children, aged five to eight, are in the zone to the west, where afternoon light prevails. **[Fig. 50]**

To enhance spatial definition without relying on walls, the roof is segmented in a series of parallel planes that incline alternately to the north and the south; these are interspersed with smaller triangular elements that tilt in opposite directions. In addition to modulating the spaces below, this multifaceted roof form enables natural light and ventilation to be admitted into the depth of the building through clerestory windows in the voids between the roof's canted surfaces. As with the Atrium School, it was deemed important to maintain visibility of the building systems—its distinct wall and roof segments, windows, and doors to the play yards, as well as its scuppers spewing rainwater. The freedom to manipulate the roof structure entailed a further benefit, promoting consciousness of the daily passage of the sun or the vagaries of inclement weather throughout the interior, so that the building functions as a threshold between earth and sky.

Operating in counterpoint to the spatial partitioning implied by the slanting roof planes is the series of occupiable thresholds that link the open sequence of volumes and lead ultimately to the out of doors. Distinct areas for science/art, math, language, and reading are provided for each age group. They are subdivided by mobile shelving units with open backs that operate like veils—both allowing and obscuring views of activities in

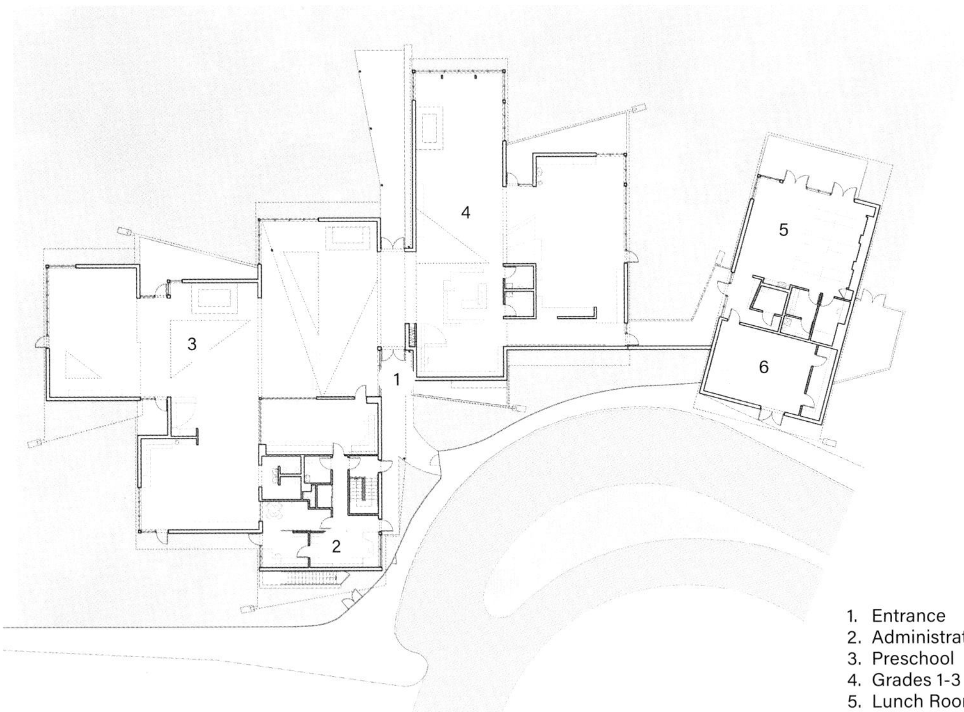

1. Entrance
2. Administration
3. Preschool
4. Grades 1-3
5. Lunch Room
6. Music Room

Figure 49 The Children's School, plan

Figure 50 The Children's School, teaching area for five to eight-year-olds

adjoining areas. **[See Fig. 115]** There are spaces of intimacy and spaces for group activities, moments of stasis as well as inducements for exploration. Each age group has a recessed forum, a gathering space for songs, games, and storytelling, bounded on three sides by rows of steps. The floor is carpeted for sound absorption, although the students are typically so immersed in their activities that the building is remarkably quiet. In-floor heating encourages them to sprawl on the carpet to do their work, with guidance from the staff, who sit level with the children on the floor. To provide acoustical separation for noisy activities, an adjoining structure, reached by a covered walkway, contains multipurpose spaces for gross motor skills/lunchroom and a dance/music room. A separate art barn is located in the garden.

Unlike the meandering corridor in the Atrium School, which was devised to accommodate a range of activities, the Children's School has two corridors that are straight and relatively lacking in programmatic content. These facilitate the child's transition from one environment to another. The first marks the threshold between the two principal zones of the school; it leads from the covered entry portico, where each child is greeted at the automobile drop off point by a staff member and escorted into the building, to a second covered walkway and play area to the south. This corridor serves an important function at the start of each school day; its low ceiling and visual connection to the out of doors impart an ambiance of calm to relieve any sense of separation anxiety as the child proceeds with her greeter to an adjoining area where the children assemble prior to embarking on their individual ventures. The second corridor serves as a gallery for the display of student artwork, celebrating the idea of the child as a producer of knowledge. It extends from a zone of quiet self-absorption to one that accommodates

more boisterous group activities—from the open space of the library to an external covered passage that passes by a science garden before it terminates in the ancillary structure. [See Fig. 106]

In accordance with the understanding of "child development as ever-expanding spheres of independence," an integral aspect of the school's pedagogic mission is ease of access to the external environment.[2] As Skutch noted, it was important "to acknowledge the natural world as a continuing aspect of the child's experience," while simultaneously affording the security of shelter.[3] Toward that end, each teaching area has one or more doors leading directly to a one-acre fenced-in play yard. The transition from building to yard is mediated by roof overhangs above wooden decks that are used for outdoor activities during inclement weather, when the rainwater that plunges from roof scuppers is collected in barrels. [Fig. 51] Rainfall is thus celebrated both as a source of audible and visual delight and as nourishment for the garden—an activity in which the students participate by using the hose attached to each barrel to water the lawns. Whereas the youngest children are confined to the fenced-in portion of the site, which is equipped with a large sandpile, the older ones are encouraged to wander further afield to experience the invigorating and restorative power of the natural environs. Although their activities are closely monitored, this might involve taking a book out to the lawn to read in the sunshine, satisfying their creative instincts in the art barn, or using the circle of upright tree stumps in the wooded portion of the site to participate in group activities.

The Children's School was one of the first schools in Connecticut to be LEED-certified by the U.S. Green Building Council. Passive means of energy conservation include the building's primary southern orientation; its concrete slab construction to provide thermal mass; sunshades and overhangs to afford protection from the summer sun while admitting the heat from the low-lying winter sun; and operable windows to facilitate cross ventilation, amplified by ceiling fans, which obviates the need for air conditioning.

Finish materials were selected to buttress the school's pedagogical objectives. To enhance visual connections with the site's wooded environs, Western red cedar, used as the primary facade material, was extended into the soffits of the entry thresholds and the two corridors. Interior walls are painted white to provide a canvas for the play of natural light that emanates from the clerestory windows and draws attention to the bright colors and textural variety of the learning materials, which are variations on those formulated by Maria Montessori. Each forum space has a wall of porcelain whiteboard for use as a drawing surface, while selected wall segments are covered in floor-to-ceiling mirrors to expand the space visually and draw the children's attention to the theatricality of their movements.

The Children's School cannot be understood as a discrete object. Instead, Thompson envisaged the complex as a field condition in which the subjective experience of the child is prioritized. Throughout the building, students are oriented to the natural conditions of the broader landscape by architectural means: vertically, through clerestory windows, to the daily path of the sun and to temporal weather conditions, and horizontally, via a sequence of occupiable thresholds, to the out of doors—the play yards, and the woodlands beyond.

Early Learning Center for Novartis Pharmaceuticals Corporation, East Hanover, NJ (2012–15)

The integral relationship of building and landscape was also a primary factor in Thompson's next early education facility—a 20,000 square-foot daycare center for the infants and preschool children of workers at the North American headquarters of Novartis Pharmaceuticals Corporation. [Fig. 52] When Thompson was awarded the commission, no daycare provider had been designated. This afforded an opportunity to further her pursuit of architectural means

2 Dr. Jules Spotts cited by Maureen Murphy, blog post, "Dr. Jules Spotts on Separation," 28 August 2016, childrensschool.org. accessed June 21, 2020

3 Skutch and Hamlin, "Environmental Flexibility for Preschoolers" (1975): 326.

Figure 51 The Children's School, covered external decks

to address the pedagogical issues associated with early childhood education, with the encouragement of Board Chairman Daniel Vasella, whose personal interest in architecture led to his active involvement in the design process.[4]

This was Thompson's first commission to design a building solely for children of this age group. She began by visiting a daycare center operated by Bright Horizons, a nationwide provider of employer-sponsored child care facilities founded in 1986. Unlike The Children's School, these programs have separate classrooms for the different age groups to assist in noise mitigation, particularly during naptime. Moreover, although daily outdoor excursions comprise a fundamental aspect of the Bright Horizons program, these usually involve time spent in a conventional playground or walks in the immediate environs, rather than in outdoor spaces envisaged as integral components of the learning environment—a quality Thompson explicitly sought to incorporate in her design.

Thompson and her team developed schematic designs for three different sites. Two were variations on courtyard schemes amid the office complex. Only the third option, on a gently sloping wooded plot of land that terminates a major axis through the office and research buildings, afforded an opportunity to achieve a more comprehensive synthesis of building and landscape, and it quickly earned Vasella's approval. In a layout that he associated with "airplane wings taking off," Thompson fragmented the building volume to break down its scale in a manner appropriate to young children and foster their engagement with the natural environs. [Figs. 53 & 54] Splayed out from a central system of ramps and open spaces for group activities are

4 Daniel Vasella was CEO of Novartis (1996–2010) and chairman of the Board of Directors (1999–2013); he granted final approval of the design just prior to his departure from the company.

Figure 52 Early Learning Center for Novartis Pharmaceuticals, East Hanover, viewed from the company offices

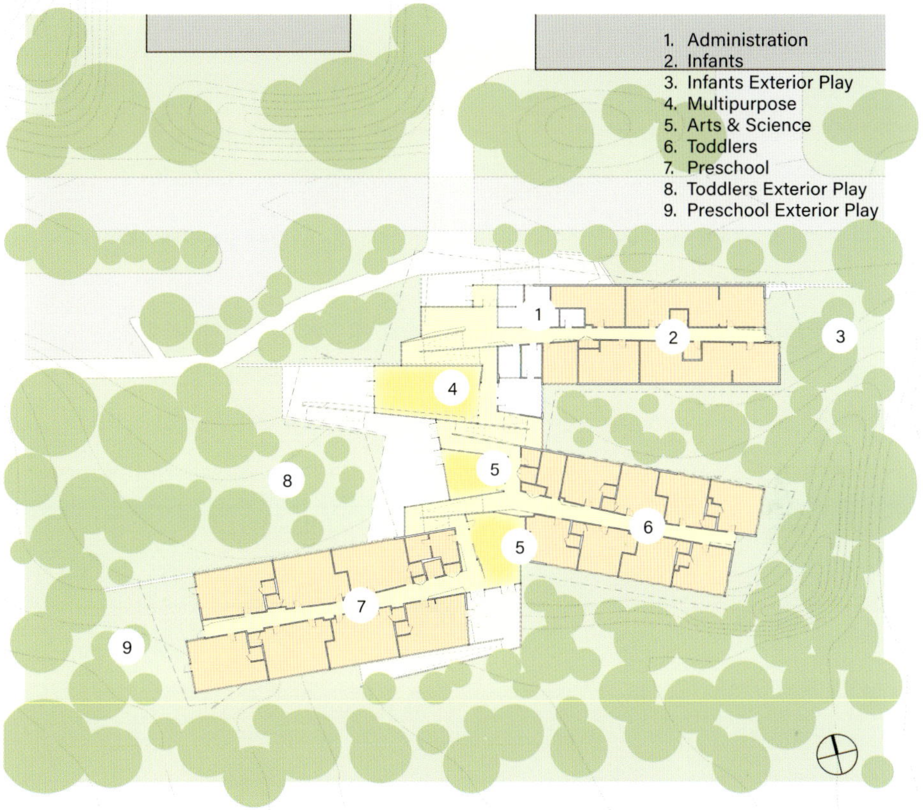

single-story wings of classrooms for each age group that extend into the landscape, just as landscape elements penetrate the open areas between them. Each wing culminates in a fenced-in garden or play yard that overlooks the woodland beyond.

The ramp, a formal device that Thompson first used at the Atrium School, is now a primary feature of the learning environment. The ramps that link the discrete classroom levels of the Novartis facility begin in the entry lobby and extend alternately to the east and the west, so that each switchback affords a view to a different landscape. Negotiating this system of tilted ground planes augments the children's bodily awareness in relation to the slope of the land, enhancing their kinesthetic sense of spatial dynamics accrued by the body in motion and transforming the entire sequence into an indoor playground.

Amplifying the civic nature of this central zone are collective spaces arrayed at the base of each ramp. **[Fig. 55]** A generous entrance lobby is followed by an open multipurpose volume at the next level, which accommodates group activities outside the classrooms, including lunchtime for the older children. Occupying the final two levels are art/science classrooms for the toddlers and the preschool students respectively. Equipped with sinks to provide water for projects and for cleanup, they are bounded by glass partitions to facilitate the children's awareness of the activities taking place within these classrooms while maintaining visibility of the adjoining landscape. The combination of windows to the classrooms with those to the external environs gives this central zone the atmosphere of an urban street, reinforcing its civic essence and contributing to a sense of ambiguity between interior and exterior, building and landscape. **[Fig. 56]**

To assist with developing the schematic design and elaborate upon the gardens

Figures 53 & 54
Early Learning Center for Novartis Pharmaceuticals: site concept diagram; plan diagram

and play yards, Thompson brought in her frequent collaborator, landscape architect Van Valkenburgh, who was formulating the landscape strategy for the east campus of the Novartis headquarters (2005–15). His penchant for garden design led MVVA to take advantage of the sloping site by envisaging the fenced-in play yards as a rolling, lushly planted terrain for the children to navigate, rather than as a conventional playground. [Fig. 57] This evocation of a natural landscape in miniature includes separate areas for the infants, toddlers, and preschool children. Circuitous tracks for tricycles wind through the play yards for the toddlers and preschool children, each of which includes a miniature "village" of wooden structures. In addition to sand piles, climbing structures, and slides appropriate for each age group, there are specific learning areas—raised planting beds, "secret" paths for the children to discover, and, for the older children, a collection of natural materials and supplies for building forts. Apart from an open lawn to accommodate a variety of games, the site is densely planted to impart a sense of visual continuity with the wooded hillside, an effect aided by the use of woven wire netting for the fencing. In a manner analogous to the pedagogical value of the internal ramps, navigating this series of verdant mounds facilitates the children's kinesthetic sense of their bodies in motion.

Many aspects of the Novartis Early Learning Center are adapted from Thompson's earlier schemes: the fractured roof form and clerestory windows that mark the building as a threshold between earth and sky; covered outdoor play spaces that extend the horizontal thresholds between interior and exterior; and a profusion of operable windows that facilitate natural ventilation and minimize reliance on electric lighting. Extending well beyond the basic provision of classrooms in a typical daycare center, the open system of ramps and collective spaces imparts a lively communal ambiance to MTA's Novartis facility, evoking the Dutch architect Herman Hertzberger's notion that

Figure 55 Early Learning Center for Novatris Pharmaceuticals, lobby sitting area

Figure 57 Early Learning Center for Novartis Pharmaceuticals, view from MVVA play yards

Figure 56 Early Learning Center for Novartis Pharmaceuticals, ramped circulation zone

schools should be designed to function like cities, so that children can learn to take their place in the broader society.[5]

Princeton University Child Care Center, Princeton, NJ (2013–18)

With MTA's Child Care Center for the infants, toddlers, and preschool children of Princeton University employees and students, aspects of the Reggio Emilia philosophy were adapted to encompass the natural environs of the grounds as components of the learning environment, leading to a more explicit integration of architecture and landscape design. [Fig. 58] Reflecting upon the children's delight when they gathered in the shade of a grove of mature trees outside the existing daycare center, program director Susan Bertrand sought a more direct integration of building and landscape in the new facility. MVVA, who developed the master plan for the eastern segment of the campus, joined the design team when Thompson was engaged in planning and programming for the building. Van Valkenburgh's studies had validated the University's selection of the site for the project: a treeless expanse with a gradual slope at the easternmost end of the campus near a neighborhood of single-family houses. It provided a relatively blank canvas on which to operate. Bertrand worked with Thompson and Van Valkenburgh to expand upon aspects of the Reggio Emilia educational philosophy—in which the learning environment

Figure 58 Princeton University Child Care Center, Princeton, entrance

5 See Herman Hertzberger, *Spaces and Learning: Lessons for Students 3*, John Kirkpatrick, trans. (Rotterdam: 010 Publishers, 2008).

Figures 59 & 60
Princeton University Child Care Center: ramp to preschool wing with art room to the right; library alcove and preschool corridor viewed from the bottom of the ramp

is valued as "the third teacher"—to include novel programmatic elements as well as opportunities for the children to engage more directly in the landscape of the play yards.

The Child Care Center is bifurcated into wings for infants/toddlers and preschool students respectively, so that classrooms for ambulant children open directly to south-facing yards. The light-filled entrance lobby features an alcove lined with benches that provides parents a spot for impromptu meetings and social encounters. [See Fig. 117] Although entry further into the facility is limited to the children and staff members, a short ramp that leads down to the preschool wing affords glimpses of a book-lined reading nook and a glass-lined art room that opens to the play yards beyond—recalling the open communal zone of the Novartis Early Learning Center. [Figs. 59 & 60] Corridors in the two wings are enlivened by spaces for small group meetings or for calm respite from the busy classrooms. [See Fig. 103] Thompson enhanced spatial variety in these corridors by differentiating the heights of their canted ceiling planes and introducing skylights to admit natural light and evoke consciousness of the daily passage of the sun. Each L-shaped classroom includes a space for group activities and an alcove for individual or small group work, while a combination of operable windows and skylights facilitates cross ventilation. [Figs. 61 & 62] Other supportive elements include open storage cabinets so that supplies can be rearranged to highlight their aesthetic qualities, an idea adopted directly from Reggio Emilia educational precepts. In addition to classrooms that are tailored to the requirements of the different age groups, the building includes a dedicated art room, a multipurpose room, and a full-service kitchen. To enable the preschool children to observe the steps involved in preparing the food they eat each day and savor the associated smells, the kitchen shares a half wall with the multipurpose room.

Because of its location on the campus of a major research university, the Child Care Center is uniquely equipped to integrate early education and developmental science. At the end of the wing for infants and toddlers is a research space for professor Casey-Lew Williams, faculty member in the Department of Psychology and co-director of the Princeton Baby Lab—a vehicle for investigating how young children learn and why early learning is consequential for children's lives. With parental permission, children in the center are invited to take part in studies throughout the school year that help researchers understand how learning happens and how science can support diverse aspects of children's development.

Through conversations with Bertrand, Thompson and Van Valkenburgh conceived

Figures 61 & 62 Princeton University Child Care Center, preschool classroom; infant classroom

of the play yards as gardens. The relatively flat terrain was built up in a series of artificial mounds and laid out in a manner that draws upon the children's natural curiosity by encouraging exploration amid the open lawns and dense vegetation, where they might hide from view or even momentarily feel lost before regaining their sense of orientation. [Figs. 63 & 64] The planting includes native grasses, flowers, and trees selected to attract birds and butterflies and draw the children's attention to the changing seasons. Small seating areas provide opportunities to draw upon the pedagogical potential of natural elements and processes. For example, to enable the children to experience the full cycle of stormwater management, rainwater falling on the roof is channeled to scuppers, from which it drops onto rocks in the play yards. It then flows through dry rock stream beds to a water garden before it ends in a pond just beyond the fenced-in area, which is the catchment basin for the entire eastern segment of campus. To foster further respect for the environment, a solar panel added to the roof of a play house powers a red lightbulb so the children are made aware when the solar array is producing energy. The chain link fences that circumscribe the individual play yards are lined with shrubbery to make them less obtrusive, albeit with occasional gaps so the children can glimpse their friends or siblings in other age levels.

In addition to play houses, swing sets, and slides, several novel features in these spaces are directed to developing the children's gross motor skills: natural stone pathways to encourage jumping from rock to rock; balance bars; an artificial hill equipped with a slide; spigots fitted with cranks so the children can make the water flow; and tricycle tracks that thread though the zones for toddlers and preschool children. Other elements draw attention to natural forms and processes: moss-covered rocks; dry stream beds; raised growing beds; beach-like sandy areas bounded by large rocks; and vertical tree stumps for seating. To capitalize upon the health and psychological benefits of playing in the dirt, access from the toddler and preschool classrooms to their respective gardens is by means of shared mudrooms that are equipped with storage

Figure 64 Princeton University Child Care Center, view from play yard

for coats and boots and a sink for cleanup prior to reentry. The gardens/play yards are thus fully integrated with the architecture as essential educational components of the child care facility.

Such respect for the natural environment extends to the use of energy-saving materials and equipment as well as the passive solar design principles that Thompson draws upon in virtually all of her projects. Less visible at Princeton are many of the building's green features, such as the rooftop photovoltaic array, super-insulated walls, low-flow plumbing, and a storm-water management system, which contribute to the building's LEED Gold certification.

The complex also serves a broader civic role. In response to Bertrand's aspiration to encourage neighborhood parents to meet with their counterparts outside the school, a deep overhang at the building entrance is furnished with benches and storage for strollers and tricycles, while a tricycle path leads through a series of artificial hillocks where their children can play [Fig. 58]. The internal civic zone first developed at the Novartis Early Learning Center is here externalized as a site of public engagement.

Figure 63 MVVA, Princeton University Child Care Center, landscape concept plan

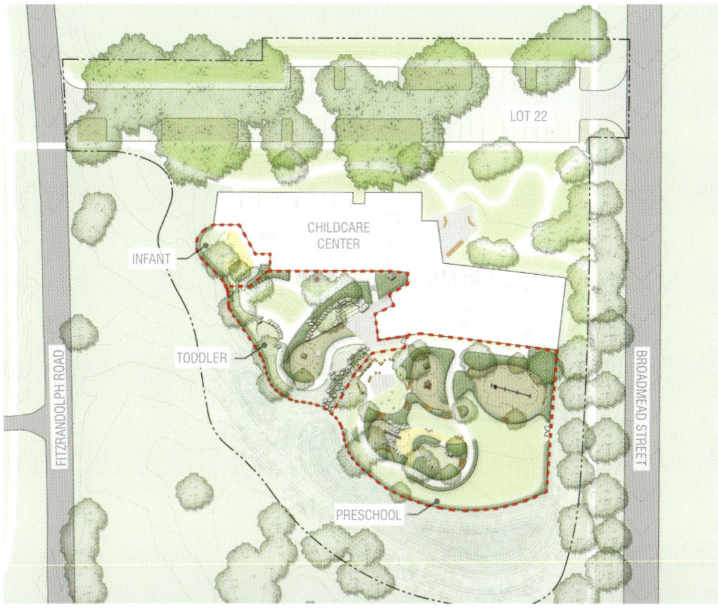

MGM Head Start and Family Center, Springfield, MA (2017–18)

In common with other former industrial centers in the region, Springfield, Massachusetts had fallen into decline during the second half of the twentieth century. Thompson's MGM Head Start and Family Center is part of an extensive effort by MGM Resorts International to revitalize the urban environs in hopes of boosting the local economy by attracting tourists to its extensive recreational venues. MTA's building is intended to serve children from the city's lowest income families. Despite severe site and budget constraints, Thompson was able to address pedagogic objectives similar to those of her other early learning facilities while achieving zero energy certification for the project.

Located in a former industrial zone bounded by apartment buildings and single-family houses, the constricted site lies between two low-rise buildings and an adjoining parking lot. This necessitated a compact building configuration in which Thompson optimized the energy-collecting potential of the rooftop photovoltaic panels by subdividing the roof into two parallel inclined planes. [Fig. 65] The 5,500-square-foot structure includes four classrooms—one for infants and three for preschool children—along with a dedicated parental support space, which reflects the significant role that parents play in the child's emotional and intellectual development. The classrooms open directly to south-facing playgrounds for the respective age groups, which are outfitted with standard, commercially available equipment and sparse planting. To impart consciousness of the natural environs, the classrooms have large banks of windows that overlook the playgrounds, while clerestories spanning between the roof planes admit soft northern light and facilitate cross-ventilation.

Figure 65 MGM Head Start and Family Center, Springfield

Figures 66 & 67
MGM Head Start and Family Center: entry lobby; corridor

Directly inside the lobby is a bench for impromptu meetings among teachers and parents, which supplements the dedicated meeting room down the hall. [Fig. 66] These spaces accommodate parents who wish to spend private time with their children during occasional breaks in their work schedules, meet with the teachers, or attend nighttime parenting classes. Augmenting the natural light admitted at either end of the corridor are alternating diagonal ceiling fixtures disposed along its length. Low benches and cubby storage units are provided for the children. Bright colors on the floors, walls, and soffits of the corridor and classrooms contribute to the center's welcoming atmosphere. [Fig. 67]

Energy-saving devices extend beyond those in MTA's previous commissions of this type. They include geothermal HVAC and photovoltaic electric systems, triple-paned windows, and lighting controlled by occupancy and daylight sensors, which enabled the center to achieve LEED platinum certification and fulfill the stringent guidelines for zero energy certification from the International Living Future Institute.

◆◆◆

With these commissions MTA probes the role that architecture can play not only as an essential component of early childhood education but also as a potential civic amenity. While bringing joy to the daily lives of the children, their teachers, and their caregivers, these projects instill respect for the natural environment and for the conservation of natural resources. At the same time, they demonstrate the value of reaching out to the broader community—whether by opening playgrounds to the neighborhood, as at the Atrium School, encouraging impromptu encounters among neighborhood parents and their children, as in Princeton, or providing direct services to the public, as in Springfield.

Figure 68 Overleaf
The Children's School, Stamford, view from the west

Shantel Blakely

Creature Comforts: A Sensibility for Tectonic Expression

I first met Maryann Thompson during my freshman year at Harvard. She was the teaching assistant for Eduard Sekler's architectural history course, where she led a small discussion section and operated the slide projectors. To illustrate his lectures Sekler used not only 35mm slides, some of which he had photographed himself, but also several 4×5-inch glass plates that were loaded individually into a large projector. That projector, when I glimpsed it in the Carpenter Center projection booth, looked like a magic lantern. In spite of the chaos of my undergraduate life, I was spellbound by that class. I sat quietly among the first year M.Arch. students and mimicked them in sketching from the slides. Some students dozed off (and, after working with two of them on a group assignment, I understood why), but I listened attentively as Sekler spoke from the podium in the dark lecture hall. In what he called "tectonic expression" in buildings, the arrangement of structural elements could appear to be as precise as clockwork, as forceful as a contact sport, and as cerebral as a chess game. I would later associate Thompson's architecture projects with this idea. I became more fully acquainted with her work when I returned to Cambridge not long after completing my M.Arch. degree and worked for her, first at Thompson and Rose and then at her own firm. Consciously or unconsciously, she seems to have internalized Sekler's conceptual framework as a way of thinking about architecture, which makes the concept of tectonic expression useful as a means to understand her architectural sensibility.

In "Structure, Construction, and Tectonics," an essay that appeared in György Kepes's anthology *Structure in Art and in Science* (1965), Sekler defines tectonic expression by differentiating among three interrelated concepts. Whereas he understands "structure" to be the "system or principle of arrangement destined to cope with forces at work in a building, such as post-and-lintel, arch, vault, dome, and folded plate, ... [c]onstruction," he maintains, is "the concrete realization" of a structural technique in wood, stone, metal, or other materials. On the tectonic Sekler writes:

> When a structural concept has found its implementation through construction, the visual result will affect us through certain expressive qualities which clearly have something to do with the play of forces and corresponding arrangement of parts in the building, yet cannot be described in terms of construction and structure alone. For these qualities, which are expressive of a relation of form to force, the term tectonic should be reserved.[1]

1 Eduard Sekler, "Structure, Construction, Tectonics," in *Structure in Art and in Science*, György Kepes, ed. (New York: George Braziller, 1965), 89–95, here 89. This book was the first volume of the "Vision + Values" series of publications edited by György Kepes, which featured lectures that had been given in his seminars at MIT.

Thus, form may either be congruent with static structural requirements—in which the shape of a member follows the diagram of support that is needed to resist gravity—or it may not reveal the structural diagram at all. Sekler made it clear that architects have broad discretion here. They must operate between the requirements of structural adequacy and the enticements of freely shaped form, but just how they negotiate this range of possibilities will characterize their work and distinguish it from that of other architects. Tectonic expression is accordingly the manner in which an architect conveys a structural "story," or the apparent performance of its physical system, to the human observer.

Sekler considered tectonic expression to be compelling in interiors as well as in the general building form. Discussing the Great Room of the Palais Stoclet in Brussels, for example, where Joseph Hoffmann created a double-height volume

Figure 69 Josef Hoffmann, Palais Stoclet Great Room, Brussels (1905–11)

that is bounded by marble-clad columns, Sekler explained how the height of the space is emphasized by the visibility of those columns, which appear to support both the mezzanine and the ceiling. [Fig. 69] This interpretation of the columns' structural role might not actually be true. In the view cited above, the columns on the right appear to be identical to those on the left, but close inspection reveals that those below the left side of the mezzanine are partly embedded in a wall. For all we know, that wall might be load-bearing, as might the walls beyond the mezzanine. What matters from a tectonic point of view is not the truth about the structural forces at play in the volume but the impression that this set of columns makes on the observer, namely that the columns apparently hold up the ceiling. Hoffmann created this effect by making sure that a portion of each column remains in front of the parapet so that its full length is exposed to view. During his lecture, Sekler would run the rubber tip of a long wooden pointer up and down against the screen to trace the columns' full, uninterrupted height.

Figure 70 Thompson and Rose, Leeper Studio Complex, Atlantic Center for the Arts, New Smyrna Beach, painting and sculpture studios

Figures 71 & 72 Walden Pond Visitor Center, Concord: principal entry facade; array of columns on deck

Thompson's projects are replete with such moments in which, as she puts it, "the viewer is in a didactic relationship with the way the building is being held up and supported."[2] In her work, as in Hoffmann's, a building might be an unreliable narrator. In the Leeper Studio Complex at the Atlantic Center for the Arts (Thompson and Rose, 1989–97), for instance, each pavilion is fashioned as a wooden shed, but the scale and height of these sheds exceeds what could be realized with wood alone. The loadbearing is achieved by a combination of concrete base walls and concealed steel columns as well as occasional exposed wooden trusses. [Fig. 70] This structural complexity imparts an air of enchantment to these buildings; the roofs appear as though frozen in place while being pulled upward by some unseen but powerful force.

The Walden Pond Visitor Center (2011–16) is another example of a heterogeneous, playfully ambivalent structural system. The single-story volume is made primarily of wood, and the facade toward the pond is mostly glass, with clerestory windows above its large, wood-framed sliding doors. The roof slopes upward as it extends to the overhang over an adjoining wooden deck, where a row of slim columns in galvanized steel aligns with the wooden supports in the facade to give partial support to the overhang. [Figs. 71 & 72] In addition to its role as a literal armature, this row of steel columns lends itself to other impressions. In certain weather conditions, the columns, being thinner than the adjacent wooden columns and light gray in color, blend into the sky

2 Maryann Thompson, email correspondence to the author, 19 September 2021.

behind them. As a result, the roof appears to be dramatically cantilevered. These columns are part of an array of steel members, which includes shorter columns of the same diameter that support an adjoining trellis of natural locust beams. The steel columns *en masse* establish a field of vertical lines that appears to shimmer in the sunlight; yet because they are visually subordinate to the wooden supports, they are easily overlooked, just as sticks and wires on a marionette may go unseen without being invisible.

Thompson's interest in developing a building design to create particular impressions of loadbearing suggests a fundamental sensitivity to materials, space, atmospheric conditions, and structural forms as resources that can be perceived as meaningful by the human observer. She centers the human interpreter of buildings as the subject of her architectural interventions, just as Sekler does with his emphasis on tectonic expression.

Further support for this way of thinking about architecture can be found in Charles Eames' comments on "goods," or materials that are capable of being transformed by the architect, and in John Dewey's concept of the "live creature," an individual who is adept at identifying such goods and gauging their potential. Eames, who, like Sekler was a friend and collaborator of György Kepes, expounds on goods in an eponymous short film of 1971. In the aftermath of a burglary, he explains in a voiceover, "[e]verything in Ray's car had been strewn all over the lot," yet much that the family valued had been left behind. Walking around, picking up their possessions, the couple found a bolt of cloth. "It was a bolt of wool," Eames explains, "When you take hold of it, why, you can feel the animal wax and oil in it somehow or other. A great bolt of cloth.... What was shocking about it was that the guy hadn't thought enough of it to take it...."[3] As exemplified by the cloth, "goods" are materials whose possession confers other desirable capacities.

The "live creature," Dewey explains in *Art as Experience* (1934), is exemplified by an animal—a fox, a dog, or a thrush, for example—that is alert to the panoply of experiences that come through all of its senses. It singles out whatever is strongly affecting and commits it to memory. Its actions anticipate and respond to these things and associations. Dewey writes, "The live animal is fully present, all there, in all of its actions: in its wary glances, its sharp sniffings, its abrupt cocking of ears...." For the artist, too, things in the world are bound up with values such as security, comfort, wonder, or awe. As

3 A transcript of "Goods" (1971), which was screened in Eames's Norton Lectures delivered at Harvard University in the 1970–71 academic year, appears in Charles and Ray Eames, *An Eames Anthology*, Daniel Ostroff, ed. (New Haven and London: Yale University Press, 2015), 307–08.

Dewey elaborates, the artist-as-live-creature perceives whatever is valuable in the jumble of a life that is marked by aesthetic experience; the work of art is a confection composed of such things. The existence of art gives Dewey hope for humanity, for it proves that the human, like other animals, has the capacity "of restoring consciously, and thus on the plane of meaning, the union of sense, need, impulse, and action characteristic of the live creature."[4] As I read Sekler, tectonic expression is a corresponding practice in architecture. The architect uses physical and spatial experiential goods as raw materials for the design—an artwork that is meaningful because of its visible relationships of form and force, which is further validated by the percipient observer.

4 John Dewey, *Art as Experience* (New York: Minton, Balch & Co., 1934), 19, 25.

Thompson's facility with tectonic expression is distinctly evident in her building renovations, where her interventions are perceived in relation to existing architectural goods or conditions. The Fayerweather Street House (1998–2002), a project I worked on at Thompson and Rose as well as in Thompson's independent practice, shows how she can bring a new character to an existing building by disclosing its latent architectural goods and amplifying them to generate new experiences. A spacious single-family residence, the Fayerweather Street House was created by repurposing an existing primary school building in Huron Village, a Cambridge neighborhood of modest three-story homes. While the school was tucked deep inside the block and barely noticeable from the adjacent streets, it was a sizeable building with a Brutalist sensibility, owing to its structural concrete frame and facades of brick infill panels and floor-to-ceiling windows. The grid of columns provided an open floorplan with high-ceilinged rooms and a fully glazed south-facing garden facade, but the abundant concrete surfaces and floor slabs harbored deep shadows.

Figure 73 Fayerweather Street House, Cambridge, entry hall

In the entry foyer, Thompson placed wood panels on the walls. Between flagstones added to the floor, she inserted smooth, matte, asphalt-colored stones that the occupants and their visitors would sense underfoot. [Fig. 73] The stones' rounded shapes and saturated color create a lively pattern of light and shadow, in counterpoint to the maple panels and refurbished segments of smooth polished concrete. This use of natural materials in the foyer seamlessly continues the dialogue with the site that begins in the garden, where Michael Van Valkenburgh replaced an existing driveway with a grove of white birch trees and a field of small purple flowers traversed by staggered paving stones. The sensory impressions add up as one ventures further into the house, where Thompson made a series of interventions to take advantage of the height and volume of the original Fayerweather Street School building.

The hallway that leads from the foyer to the back of the house affords selected views of the garden through large windows introduced to either side. A slot cut through the soffit overhead, crossed by concrete beams that remain

Figure 74 Fayerweather Street House, Great Room

in place, allows the entry sequence to be punctuated by light and sound from above. The route culminates in a Great Room to the left and an open kitchen to the right. [Fig. 74] The main transformative gesture in this expansive space is a large excision from the concrete waffle slab above the Great Room. On the back facade, where an expanse of glass extends the full two stories in height, the edge-beam of the second-floor slab remains visible from the garden, as though nothing was changed. On the inside this deep beam is lined with wood; from the Great Room it looks like a giant mullion and does nothing to undermine the impression of total transparency.

Figure 75 Fayerweather Street House, mezzanine over Great Room

Thompson was not content with a mere balcony overlook at the second level; instead, she introduced a pair of metal walkways to either side of the double height volume. [Fig. 75] These extend beyond the rear facade to a pair of decks that hover over the back yard. Whether looking up from the first floor or down from the mezzanine, viewing out to the garden, or sensing the natural light that suffuses the interior, the visitor can revel in the room's scale from many positions within it. The impression of continuity between the Great Room and the great outdoors, crucial to this design, is sustained in part by these walkways, whose metal armature makes them appear lightweight while their floors are made of the same water-resistant wood that is used on the decks of their outdoor extensions. The Great Room is thus transformed from a luxury amenity into a thing of intrinsic value, analogous in its plenitude of experiences to Eames's bolt of cloth.

In some of Thompson's designs, tectonic expression extends beyond a particular set of structural components to the roof, and in effect, to the entire building. At the Children's School in Stamford (2003–07), the roof resembles a pile of tilted plates reminiscent of folded sheets of paper or metal, with small dormers whose windows are triangular, like a flat surface that has been sliced and folded. [See Fig. 48] Although the building is articulated as a sequence of offset, interlocking volumes, the angles of inclination of its sheet-like roofs intersect in triangular clerestory windows. At selected corners of the building, these clerestories are continuous with floor-to-ceiling glass walls. As a result, the internal facades can be read either as solid walls capped by expanses of glass or as glass walls that extend to the ceiling, where they are protected by a combination of external wooden louvers and overhanging roofs. [Fig. 76] There is minimal evidence of the structural system at the building perimeter, where the steel supports are covered in wooden trim that is painted white to match the window mullions. A single exposed steel column, positioned at a juncture of the roof's secondary folds, provides the only overt evidence of support. The youngest students at the Children's School spend the bulk of their days sprawled upon carpeted and heated floors in this part of the building. From that vantage point they can glance up at the creases in the ceiling that correspond to the folds on the roof's outer surface. Their impression of the roof, propped up by that slim, solitary column, exemplifies what Thompson has called "the visual sense of being supported and also knowing how."[5]

As Sekler explains, "Through tectonics, the architect may make visible, in a strong statement, that intensified kind of experience of reality which is the artist's domain—in our case the experience of forces related to forms in a building."[6] In the above designs, as in many others, Thompson affirms this understanding of the architect as an artist. She uses tectonic expression to orient the user, and through this orientation she brings the observer's attention not only to goods employed in the design but also to those in the immediate vicinity. These may range from impressions of the buildings themselves to phenomena beyond them, especially in their gardens and landscapes. In this regard, Thompson's approach is close in spirit to Dewey's notion of art—not as a phenomenon that is limited by institutional definitions but as experience; and experience is everywhere. From that corner with the column in the Children's School, a child might gaze into the garden through the glass walls, which resemble sheer curtains hanging almost to the floor, and something as small as a bird alighting on a branch or a breeze that ruffles the blades of grass on the lawn might catch the eye and be made known. The image of the propped-up roof canopy could

5 Thompson, Ibid.

6 Sekler, "Structure, Construction, Tectonics" (1965), 92.

become a symbol for such experiences that infiltrate the lives that are lived for a while in that room. Such forms comprise only conventional provisions of architecture, yet in their accumulation they are often beautiful, or even magical.

Figure 76 The Children's School, Stamford, open teaching area

Part II
Themes

Site Planning

A propensity to conceive of each project as a fragment of a larger idea is a fundamental aspect of Maryann Thompson's approach to her architectural commissions, whether cultural institutions, recreational venues, schools, or private residences. Accordingly, site planning plays a significant role in her design process. She derives the entry sequence, massing, and layout of her buildings from the distinct attributes of their settings, including their topography, vegetation, orientation to the sun and prevailing winds, and opportunities for vistas.

Thompson begins each architectural commission with an analysis of the solar angles of incidence and the prevailing winds on the site at different times of the year. [Figs. 77–79] Although the relevance of these analyses for site planning is most evident in her work on open, rural sites, they pertain equally to her designs for more constricted urban locales. At the **Temple Ahavat Achim** in Gloucester (2009–12), for example, she devised the deeply layered entry facade to afford protection from the harsh winter winds that arise from the north, while admitting the cooling summer breezes that emanate from the west. [See Fig. 28] A covered open-air passage occupies the depth of the facade. As congregants enter the building, it provides shelter from the summer sun and exposes them to warming solar rays in winter. The implications of thinking at the scale of the urban environment are also evident in the interior. The processional sequence culminates in a large sanctuary space on the upper level, where clerestory windows above the Torah ark frame views of the cupolas and clocktower atop Gloucester City Hall.

In rural settings, Thompson often conceives of her buildings as subordinate to their more naturalistic sites. At the **Walden Pond Visitor Center** (2011–16), the pedestrian entry sequence focuses on the pond rather than the building. She strategically positioned her Visitor Center opposite a facsimile of Henry David Thoreau's cabin so that as visitors approach from the parking lot the open landscape between the two structures frames the view to the pond. [Fig. 80] The natural landscape also dominates at **The Oaks** (2007–13), a private residence on Martha's Vineyard. Thompson was inspired by the ephemeral quality of the dappled light that penetrates the canopy of a vast oak grove and falls on the forest floor of mosses and ferns. She worked with Michael Van Valkenburgh to configure the winding entry drive so that the presence of the house is barely discernible through the trees. [Fig. 81]

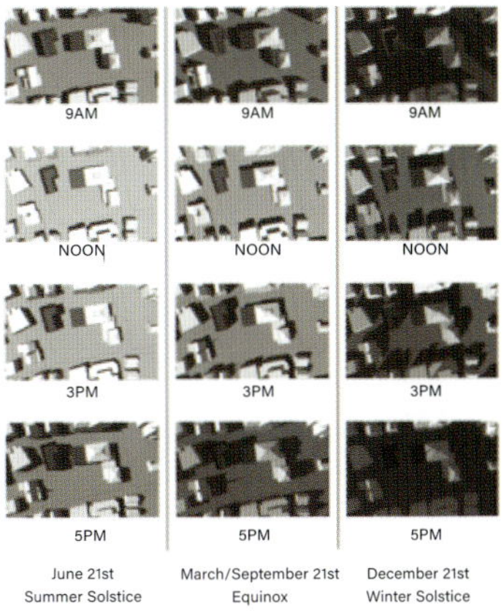

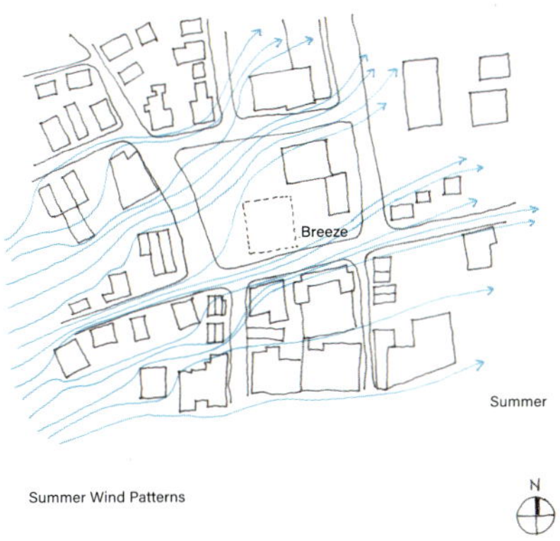

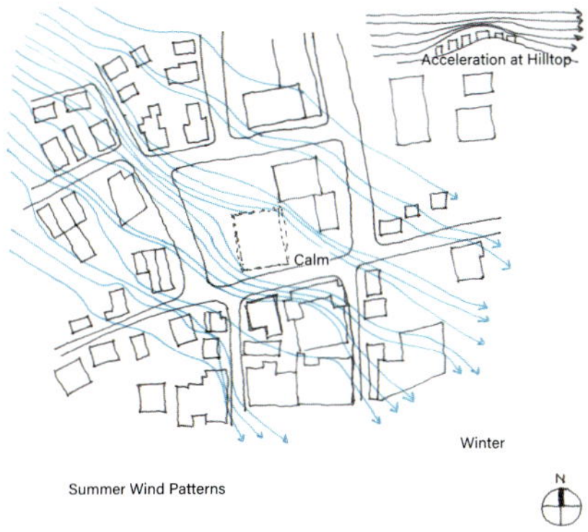

Figures 77–79 Temple Achavat Achim, Gloucester, solar impact diagrams, prevailing wind diagrams

Figure 80 Walden Pond Visitor Center, Concord, site plan

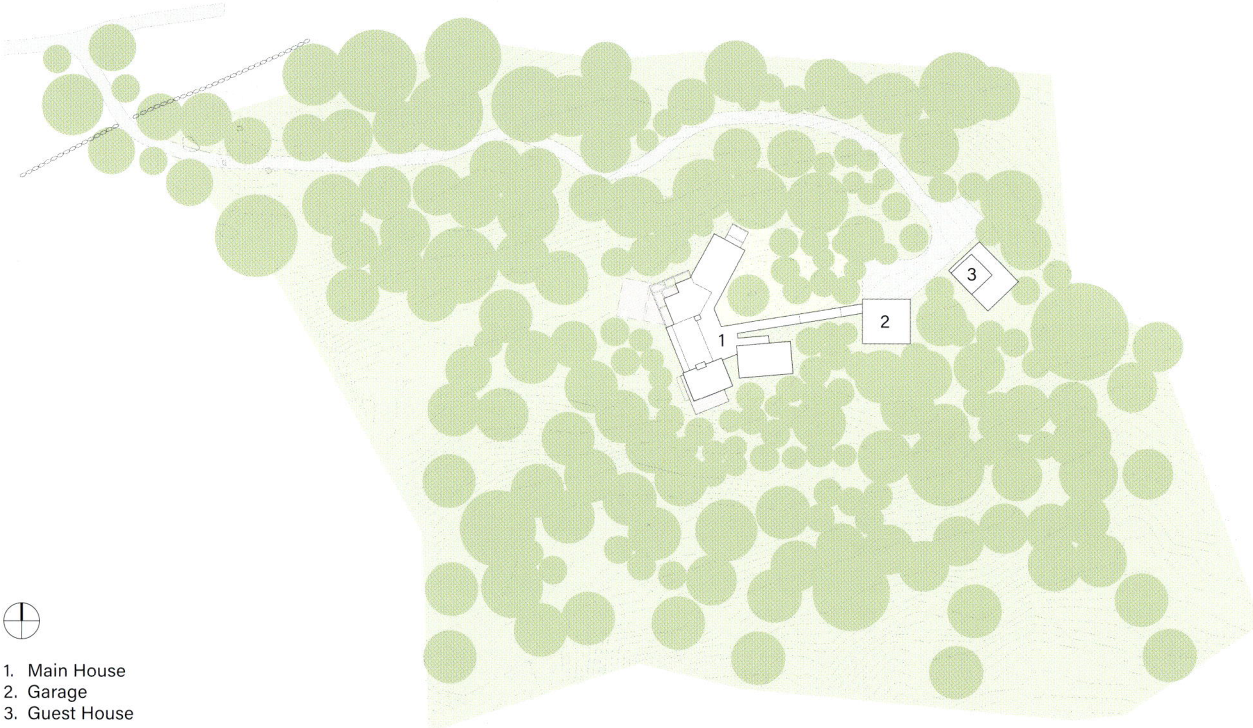

Figure 81 The Oaks, West Tisbury, site plan

The route ends in a parking area with a view to a knoll planted with aspens around which the house is configured. The immersive experience in the densely wooded environs is followed by a sense of partial emergence into a clearing as one ascends the covered pedestrian walkway that leads past the knoll to the building entrance. **[Fig. 82]** This sense of a sequence modulated by natural light is echoed in the interior, where roof overhangs limit the sunlight that is admitted into the principal living space through large wood-framed sliding glass doors surmounted by a zone of clerestory windows. **[Fig. 83]** Rather than situate an outdoor seating area directly outside the living and dining room, Van Valkenburgh suggested that the volume open directly to a thicket of ash trees to the southwest. He added native ferns to the forest floor and advised Thompson to extend a large deck into a clearing to the northwest, which is dominated by a giant oak tree. **[Fig. 84]** The house thus functions as an expanded threshold to this sunlit glade, as the sense of immersion in the forest along the drive to the house culminates in a tranquil outdoor setting in which the architecture is wholly subsidiary to the natural environs.

Other examples, such as the **Early Learning Center for the Novartis Pharmaceutical Corporation** (2012–15), reflect Thompson's proclivity for interweaving building and site, architecture and landscape. Breaking from the orthogonal layout of the Novartis campus, Thompson positioned her structure along a wooded hillside that rises at the end of a broad pedestrian path that leads through a precinct of offices and laboratories. To instill an appreciation for the effects of nature throughout the daycare facility and its play yards and gardens, she segmented the building into four, single-story classroom wings that splay out from a central sequence of ramps and open spaces that steps up the hill. **[See Figs. 53 & 54]** This fragmentation enables the classroom wings and the landings of each ramp to open to disparate views of the gardens and play yards as they merge into the surrounding woodland. The scheme exemplifies Thompson's penchant for simultaneously working at the scale of the site and that of the building.

Figures 82–84 The Oaks: pedestrian walkway to house; living/dining room; deck adjoining large oak tree

The commission to design a new **Science and Technology Center for The Foote School** in New Haven (2009–12) led Thompson to imagine how the addition of a single building might contribute to a more extensive reorganization of the entire campus landscape. She began by creating a new vehicular entrance at the northern end of the site in order to divert automobile traffic from the adjoining residential neighborhood. To forge a link to the existing network of pedestrian pathways and open spaces that threads through the property, she created a new, open-air Middle School Center near the vehicular drop off point and configured the new building to form one of its edges. [See Fig. 36] The broad set of stairs that leads to the primary building entrance includes a generous landing that doubles as a stage for large campus events such as graduation, when the center is filled with seats for the audience.

The building layout derives from both the internal spatial requirements and the qualities of the exterior spaces formed by the architecture. [Fig. 85] A covered deck along the western facade serves as both an extension of the adjoining science classrooms and a viewing platform for activities in the playing field beyond. A large, south-facing deck on the second floor, which is similarly used as an open-air classroom, adjoins a set of terraces that step down to grade level and provide seating for informal social encounters or outdoor assembles. [See Fig. 37] There is no distinct boundary between architecture and landscape. By simultaneously developing her design at the scale of the site and that of the building, Thompson created a structure that not only serves as an integral component of the campus landscape but also forges new relationships among its parts.

Several projects exemplify Thompson's propensity to use architecture to give form to a major outdoor space. In the case of the **Visual and Performing Arts Center for the Forman School** in Litchfield, Connecticut (2015–17), for example, she subdivided the

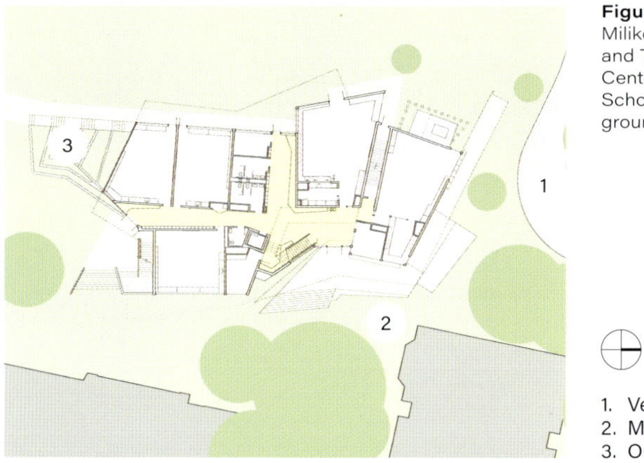

Figure 85 Jonathan Milikowsky Science and Technology Center, The Foote School, New Haven, ground floor plan

1. Vehicular Drop Off
2. Middle School Center
3. Outdoor Assembly

building program into two wings, which are linked by a central atrium and angled to give spatial definition to an academic green circumscribed by an access drive. [Fig. 86] To prioritize this new focal point for the south campus, Thompson nestled the volume of the theater into the hillside, muting the volumetric understanding of the building complex.

With her site plan for the **Lincoln Community Center** (2017–18, 2022), Thompson sought to amplify the role of landscape in the town's elementary and middle school campus. [Fig. 87] She proposed to create a new green zone off the central playing fields by dispersing the components of the new community center around its edges. To link the two outdoor spaces, she introduced wooden walkways that bridge the intervening wetlands and amplify the natural conditions of the site.

Site planning is a significant aspect of Thompson's master plans for educational institutions, in which she addresses immediate spatial requirements and the potential for future expansion. For example, MTA's master plan for the **Ethel Walker School** in Simsbury, Connecticut (2021) focuses largely on improvements to the campus environs, made through a combination of new buildings, additions and modifications to existing campus structures, and specific landscape interventions, so that the campus experience is heightened through the interrelationship of architecture and landscape. [See Fig. 168]

The recommendations include situating new buildings—residence halls and faculty housing—to configure new external spaces; redirecting vehicular circulation to the campus periphery to focus on the students' pedestrian experience; and transforming an existing retention basin into a thriving wetland ecosystem. Suggested changes to existing buildings emphasize improvements to the social aspects of the interiors and their orientation to the new gardens and landscape sequences.

Figure 86 The Forman School, Litchfield, site plan

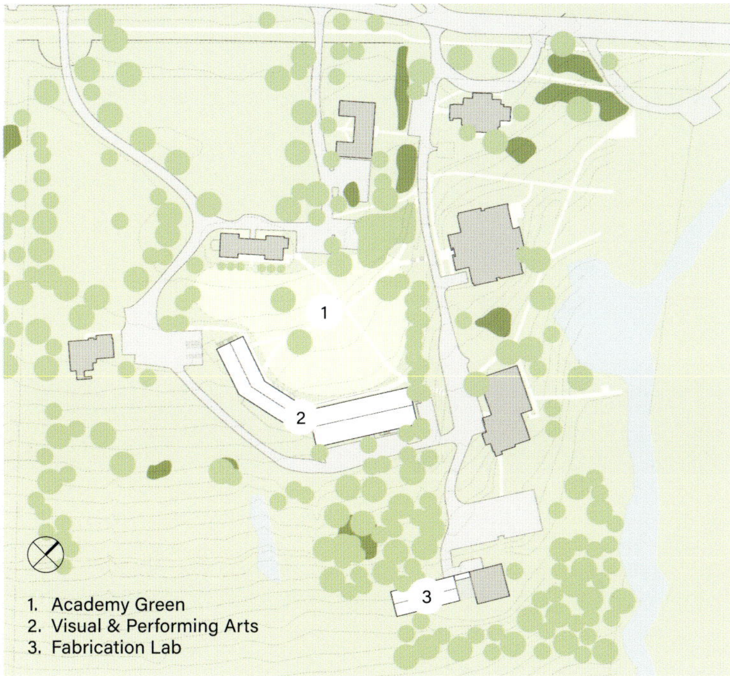

◆◆◆

A capacity for architecture to impart new meaning and value to its context, whether urban or rural, is a consistent thread in Thompson's work. Owing to the mutual inflection of site and building development throughout MTA's design process, the implications of ideas derived from the site conditions extend to all scales of a design, including the details of its formal and material systems. Moreover, three prominent themes of Thompson's architecture—the protracted entry sequence, the notion of a threshold as a spatial entity that mediates the transition from one volume to another, and the dialogue of interior and exterior—are integral to this process of operating simultaneously at the scale of the site and that of the building.

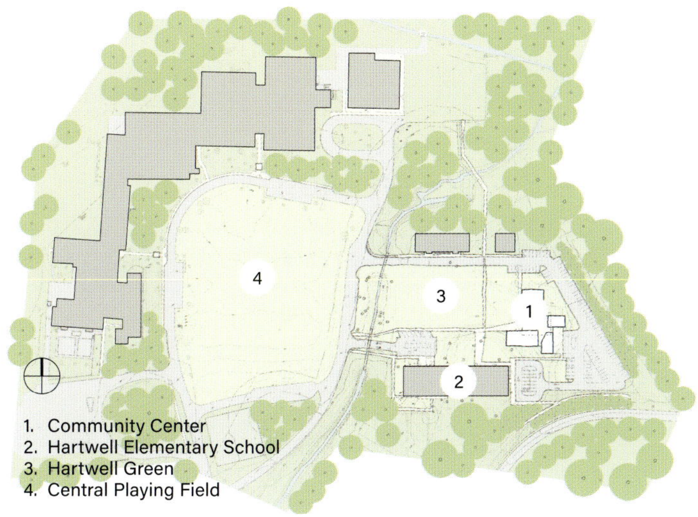

Figure 87 Lincoln Community Center, Lincoln, proposed site plan

Protracted Entry Sequence

In keeping with Thompson's attention to the interrelationship of architecture and its immediate context, whether urban or natural, protracted entry routes that take diverse forms and serve different ends characterize many of MTA's projects. These unfolding spatial sequences occur in the vehicular and pedestrian approaches to the buildings as well as their internal circulation routes. On rural sites they serve to continually reorient the occupants to relationships between the architecture, its immediate environs, distant views, and the sky. They play a further function in her public buildings—providing opportunities for impromptu social interaction.

The deep lobby/exhibition space at the **Eli and Edythe L. Broad Institute** in Cambridge (2004–06) bustles with activity throughout the day. It is fitted with seating to encourage the scientists to mingle with their colleagues from the different laboratories before they move to the bank of elevators at the back of the double-height volume. [Fig. 88 & 89] At the **Children's School** in Stamford (2003–07), in contrast, a long, low entry corridor serves as a calm space in which the children can decompress and overcome any separation anxiety as they prepare to engage in the stimulation of the learning environment.

Figures 88 & 89 Eli and Edyth L. Broad Institute, Cambridge: ground floor plan; lobby

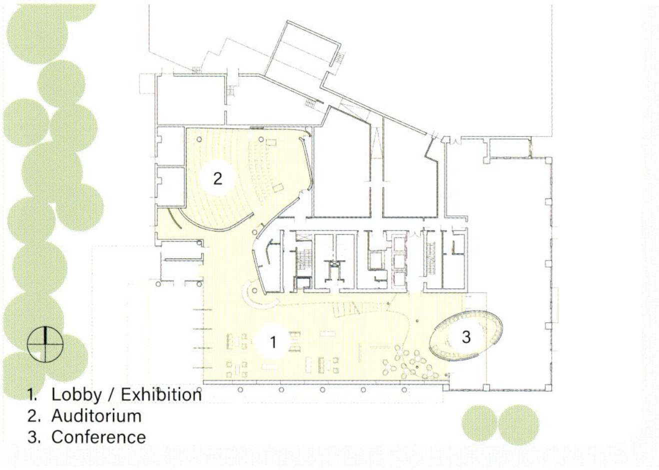

Figures 90 & 91
Temple Ahavat Achim, Gloucester: lighting effects in layered facade; external entry passage

At **Temple Ahavat Achim** in Gloucester (2009–12), the covered open-air passage that runs along the street facade serves social as well as experiential ends. It provides an opportunity for worshippers to converse with their colleagues along the entry route, where the lighting effects range from mysterious to luminous as the sun penetrates the different material conditions of the layered facade. **[Figs. 90 & 91]**

At the **Walden Pond Visitor Center** (2011–16), the pedestrian route from the parking area to the building focuses on views to the pond and surrounding landscape, which visitors might seek to experience for recreational as well as for historical reasons. **[See Fig. 80]**

On the larger sites of certain vacation houses, Thompson often extends the entry sequence to the vehicular approach, a tactic that prioritizes the landscape setting, rather than the building as an object. At **The Oaks** on Martha's Vineyard (2007–13), the presence of the house is barely discernible along the entry drive that meanders up the hilly, wooded site—a sequence on which Thompson collaborated with Michael Van Valkenburgh. The experience of the landscape remains a primary factor in the movement sequence up to and through the house, which culminates in a terrace that overlooks a magnificent ancient oak tree. **[See Figs. 81–84]**

A similar tactic resulted in a markedly different effect on the flat, open site of the **Westport Meadow House** (2002–05), which Thompson developed with landscape architect and owner Doug Reed of Reed Hilderbrand. Its low, single-story volume reaffirms the hierarchical importance of

Figure 92 Westport Meadow House, Westport, site plan

the surrounding landscape. The need to elevate the septic field on the low-lying property led Reed to position an artificial mound along the entry drive so that the house is initially visible, then momentarily concealed before it becomes fully visible on closer approach. [Fig. 92] In a similar manner, the pedestrian route from the parking area into and through the public zones of the house affords selected glimpses of the East Branch of the Westport River. These are alternately thwarted and revealed until one reaches the primary living space, where the meandering river emerges into view across the meadow. [Figs. 93–95]

◆◆◆

The protracted entry sequence is a means for Thompson to enhance the manner in which her designs inform the day-to-day experience of her buildings and their sites. Whether fostering appreciation for the transient effects of sunlight as it falls on a landscape or penetrates a building envelope, encouraging contemplation of the physical environs, or providing a locale for social or professional engagement, the entry route reflects the potential for Thompson's architecture to deflect interest to the realms of the natural and the social.

Figures 93-95 Westport Meadow House: entrance; view from entry foyer to kitchen; living/dining room with view to river.

Threshold as Liminal Condition

Figure 96 Westport Meadow House, Westport, threshold from living/dining room to covered deck on southwestern facade

Although the notion of "blurring" the boundary between interior and exterior is commonplace in architectural parlance, Thompson's work epitomizes a complex, layered, and nuanced approach to this idea. She conceives of the threshold as a three-dimensional entity that qualifies the transition from one zone to another in a manner that reflects an understanding of the boundary as a territory, rather than a line. This notion of the threshold as a liminal condition serves disparate ends. It operates at a variety of scales and in diverse circumstances: internal as well as external, vertical as well as horizontal.

Consistent with Thompson's attention to the interrelationship of building and site, this spatial concept of the threshold signifies an experiential shift at the building perimeter. She envisions the roof as well as the facades as layered entities rather than simple membranes. They mediate the transition from exterior to interior, while admitting natural ventilation and tempering natural light as it penetrates the building envelope. This contributes to a sense of ambiguity as to where the exterior ends and the interior begins, as neither interior nor exterior is prioritized.

At the **Children's School** in Stamford (2003–07), for example, Thompson modulated the form of the roof to enable natural light to penetrate the full depth of the building through triangular clerestory windows inserted between the canted roof planes. This facilitates the children's cognizance of the shifting path of the sun throughout the day, and thus their sense of place in the natural world. This elaboration of threshold in the vertical dimension is reiterated in the covered decks that extend horizontally off the multiple building entrances to form external learning spaces that mediate between the classroom zones and the surrounding play yards. [See Figs. 48, 51, 68]

The southwestern facade of the **Westport Meadow House** (2002–05) exemplifies this idea of the threshold as an entity that is layered both horizontally and vertically. Large, aluminum-framed sliding glass doors in the living/dining room open to views of the Westport River and are surmounted by operable clerestory windows. [Fig. 96] On the exterior, a narrow mahogany deck is sheltered by an overhanging roof at the height of the doors. To further mediate the afternoon sunlight that streams in from the west, Thompson extended the soffit above the clerestory windows. She brought both soffits of marine-grade mahogany into the interior. The lower one shields an enfilade of open doorways just inside the sliding glass doors, distinguishing the height of this passageway from that of the principal volume. In the upper reaches of the space, a mahogany strip that abuts the dominant white plaster surface of the ceiling demarcates the threshold zone. [See Fig. 95] This combination of formal and material gestures extends the threshold vertically as well as horizontally. The layering of the facade is amplified on the exterior by slim steel columns just beyond the sliding glass doors; these impart the suggestion of a loggia and support the roof. The perception of such a threshold is haptic as well as visual, engaging the tactility of materials, whether rough, smooth, warm, or cold. The warmth of the wood contrasts with the coolness of the glass and the steel, just as the rough surface of the wooden deck contrasts with the smooth, wooden interior flooring.

Because haptic perception is understood through bodily engagement with the physical environment—for instance, in the difference between the solidity of a floor in stone or concrete as it is sensed underfoot and the subtle give of wood flooring—the notion of the threshold as a liminal condition can similarly denote an experiential shift in an interior spatial sequence. Thompson drew upon this distinction at the **Atrium School** in Watertown (2005-06), where she marked the transition from one half level to the next with a wooden switchback ramp, positioned at right angles to the dominant flow of movement along the structure's existing concrete floor. [See Fig. 46] The shift in orientation amplifies the haptic experience of the ramp, which is sensed directly through contact with its metal handrail. At this scale, the threshold is understood as a gradation in which the kinesthetic sense of spatial dynamics accrued by the body in motion is key.

The concept of the threshold as a liminal condition can also operate at the scale of a building, serving to mediate the transition from one landscape to another and to allude to the vertical connection between ground and sky. The **Visitor Center at the Polly Hill Arboretum** on Martha's Vineyard (1991–2001) is a single room that qualifies the transition from the parking area to the arboretum landscape, while its north-facing skylight and clerestory windows draw attention to the relationship of ground to sky. [Fig. 97; see Fig. 1] A more complex variation on this idea is reflected at **The Oaks**, also on Martha's Vineyard (2007–13), where the house signifies a momentary hiatus in an experiential continuum that begins in the densely wooded condition of the site and culminates in a deck that occupies a clearing in which the presence of a vast oak tree is celebrated. [See Figs. 82–84]

◆ ◆ ◆

Thompson's understanding of the threshold as a liminal condition exemplifies her interest in creating spatial sequences envisioned in choreographic terms to elicit a bodily sense of connection to the physical environs, whether interior or exterior. She draws upon the immersive experiences of such thresholds, designed to negotiate spatial difference, to imbue her architecture with a kinesthetic sense of place.

Figure 97 Visitor Center, Polly Hill Arboretum, West Tisbury, interior

Dialogue of Interior and Exterior

Drawing upon a key concept in her work, namely the dialogue between internal spatial requirements and the particular attributes of a setting, Thompson has endowed a number of interior spaces with qualities of an exterior. This phenomenon is most evident in her vacation houses, where large sliding glass doors open fully to adjoining decks and terraces, enabling the collective family spaces to serve as seasonal screened porches. [See Figs. 185, 186, 193, 194] In two projects—the **Early Learning Center for the Novartis Pharmaceutical Corporation** (2012–15) and the **Westport Meadow House** (2002–05)—she expanded on this notion, albeit in diverse ways and for markedly different reasons. For the daycare center, Thompson imparted a civic ambiance to an open sequence of ramps and corridors by juxtaposing this circulation zone with glass-enclosed classrooms and meeting spaces, all with views to the gardens, play yards, and surrounding woodland. For the vacation house on the Westport River, in contrast, she used a variety of means to imbue the principal living spaces with the restful, ephemeral qualities of its riparian landscape setting.

The dialogue between interior and exterior at the **Novartis Early Learning Center** emanates from its massing, which Thompson fragmented in order to interweave the internal program elements with the gardens and play yards that she arrayed along the gradual slope of the site. [See Fig. 54] Single-story wings of classrooms splay out from a zone of ramps and open spaces. The children delight in negotiating the tilted ground planes of this central circulation zone, treating it as an indoor playground. Windows to the adjoining terraces and landscape elements, as well as those to a multipurpose room and the art/science classrooms, give this open sequence the character of an urban street. [Fig. 98] The resulting effect of an exterior within an interior imparts a civic dimension to the circulation zone, nurturing the children's awareness of their status as part of the broader society.

At the **Westport Meadow House**, the dialogue of interior and exterior occurs at multiple scales—in the site strategy, building layout, processional sequence, and material details. The house occupies a twenty-three-acre site that includes a large open meadow bordering a tidal estuary of the Westport River. The remnants of nineteenth-century agrarian practices and of twentieth-century mining operations left the property an uncharacteristically flat expanse. Perched at the edge of a gentle

Figure 98 Daycare Center for Novartis Pharmaceuticals, East Hanover, ramped circulation zone

slope at a point where the meadow begins its slow descent to the wetlands and the river, the house has a low, linear form that optimizes views to the water. Its layout echoes the striated layers of the site. [Fig. 99] The easternmost zone consists of a diverse collection of service spaces—the master bath, a small study, and the kitchen's counter level workspace—all oriented to take advantage of the morning light. This is followed by an open passage that traverses the full length of the house, extending through the kitchen before it terminates in an outdoor deck. An "organizing wall" that lines the far side of this passage contains storage compartments, a cinderblock fireplace, and HVAC equipment. It is sheathed in horizontal, tongue-in-groove cedar cladding to evoke specific qualities of an exterior. [Fig. 100] The density of the wall contrasts with the diaphanous qualities of the principal living spaces in the final layer—master bedroom, living/dining room, and guest room—where diagonal views through large aluminum-framed sliding glass doors extend westward to the river and the setting sun.

The entry sequence negotiates these different layers. Opposite the entrance is an outdoor sitting area that lies between the bedroom and living/dining room and overlooks a stand of trees that line the river. [Fig. 101] The sitting area serves as a threshold between the private and public zones of the house, accentuating the sense of its principal interior volumes as quasi-external spaces capable of operating as screened porches. To the left, a broad opening in the organizing wall leads to the living/dining room, which overlooks the meadow and the river.

The house is also layered vertically in a manner that corresponds to the subtle slope of the land. A concrete slab on grade in the entrance hall steps down six inches to the level of the organizing wall, where a second step leads down to the principal living spaces and adjoining wooden decks. In contrast to the grounded condition at the entry, the western side of the house seems

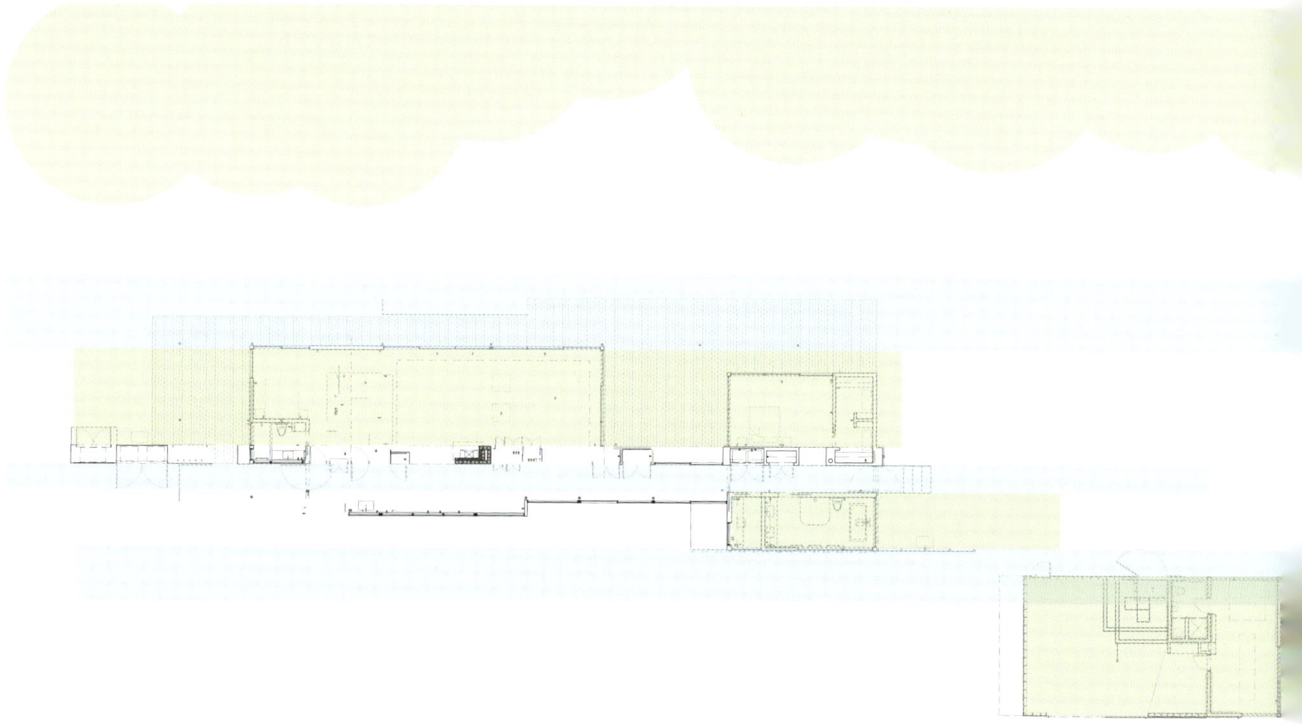

Figure 99 Westport Meadow House, Westport, plan diagram

to hover above the meadow when viewed from the direction of the river. The deck is supported on piers, which are set back from the edge and painted black to diminish their visual presence. This impression of floating is amplified by the zone of clerestory windows that surmounts the living/dining room. [Fig. 102] The combination of vertical and horizontal layering renders the boundary between interior and exterior ambiguous, a perception that is augmented by the layering of the western facade. In the living/dining room, the immediate presence of the meadow gives the volume the ephemeral character of a tent, a quality enhanced by the shifting conditions of natural light and the profusion of natural ventilation when the sliding glass doors and clerestory windows are opened. The layered, three-dimensional organization of the house is reflected in the site, where Reed created pedestrian circuits through the meadow to reach points of historic, botanic, and topographic interest in its riparian landscape.

◆◆◆

The evocation of an exterior in an interior volume enhances the occupants' consciousness of a building's relationship to its immediate environs, as well as to more distant aspects of its locale. By imparting specific qualities of an exterior to an interior volume, Thompson makes qualities of its landscape palpable, affirming her inclination to prioritize the building's setting in her designs.

Figures 100–102
Westport Meadow House: corridor with organizing wall; deck opposite entry; living/dining room

Corridors

Maryann Thompson envisions the corridor—a ubiquitous component of most school buildings that tends to be minimized in residential construction—as capable of performing multiple functions, whatever the building type. In numerous educational projects, for example, she varies the corridor widths, equips them with seating alcoves, and provides access to natural light to amplify their qualities as venues for small group meetings or solitary study.

In renovating an existing warehouse to serve as the **Atrium School** in Watertown (2005–06), Thompson expanded upon this idea. To admit daylight into every volume, she threaded the corridor around a pair of reading alcoves and classrooms of varied sizes, which are positioned according to the location of windows at the building perimeter. [See Fig. 44] A similar set of alcoves enlivens the corridors of the **Princeton University Child Care Center** (2013-18). [Fig. 103] Although Thompson's propensity to develop such corridors to accommodate multiple uses can be viewed as a budget-saving device, it serves a more significant purpose—endowing her interiors with an exhilarating sense of vitality.

A range of examples illustrates this point. The broad, U-shaped hallway at the **Chilmark Elementary School** (Thompson and Rose, 1994–2001) on Martha's Vineyard, which connects the entry hall/assembly space with the classroom wings to either side, fulfills psychological as well as practical ends. [Fig. 104] It adjoins a south-facing courtyard, so the children can benefit from regular exposure to the daily path of the sun. The hallway's thick, slab-on-grade construction provides thermal mass to absorb heat from the sun and radiate it back in the evening, thus minimizing energy consumption during the winter months, when flowering potted plants brighten the period of diminished daylight.

Figure 103 Princeton University Child Care Center, Princeton, corridor/seating alcove

Figure 104 Chilmark Elementary School, Chilmark, corridor/ assembly space

At the Science and Technology Center for The Foote School in New Haven (2009–12), the corridors are hubs of activity for much of the school day. Built-in benches enable them to serve as the seventh- and eighth-grade lounges, while doorways at both levels lead directly to outdoor decks and stairways and indirectly to diverse parts of the campus grounds, which are valued as educational milieus. [Fig. 105]

At the one-room Children's School in Stamford (2003–07), where the diverse teaching areas are linked in an open spatial sequence, Thompson introduced a pair of corridors to serve disparate ends. She conceived of the entry corridor as a calm space for the children to ease the transition from family life to their day at school. The second example, which leads from the tranquil library zone to a separate noise-filled, music/dining structure, doubles as a gallery for displaying the children's art works. [Fig. 106]

In contrast to the soothing atmosphere of The Children's School, the principal circulation zone at the Early Learning Center

Figure 105 Jonathan Milikowsky Science and Technology Center, The Foote School, New Haven, corridor/ student lounge

for Novartis Pharmaceutical Corporation in East Hanover, New Jersey (2012–15) consists of an open system of ramps and collective spaces, which the children delight in navigating, transforming this corridor-like volume into an indoor playground. [See Figs. 55, 56, 98]

At the Eli and Edythe L. Broad Institute in Cambridge (2004–06), the corridors leading to offices and laboratories are bounded by glazed partitions in order to further the interest of Institute co-founder Eric Lander in promoting an open and transparent scientific process. He initiated the idea of a "sock path"—a corridor that opens directly to offices and selected laboratories—as a means to encourage the scientists and technicians to mingle informally among themselves. [See Fig. 27]

At the Westport Meadow House (2002–05) Thompson resisted the propensity to minimize the use of corridors in residential projects in favor of celebrating their potential for forging connections between interior and exterior. An enfilade of openings just inside the western facade links the principal volume with a guest suite; it forms an implicit corridor that amplifies the threshold between inside and out. [See Fig. 96] In a more direct expression, an entry corridor that runs the full length of the plan connects the service zones with the principal living spaces. Doors at either end lead to outdoor pathways the owners developed to connect to sites of horticultural and topographic interest on their property and take advantage of its abundant river vistas. [See Figs. 94, 100]

◆ ◆ ◆

Whether enhancing the relationship between interior and exterior or directed to social, psychological, or pedagogic ends, the various iterations of corridors in Thompson's work exemplify her interest in creating spaces in which a broad range of activities might occur. As evidenced by the young children who grasped the opportunity to advance their kinesthetic sense of spatial dynamics in the sequence of ramps and open spaces at the Novartis Early Learning Center, this type of extra-functionality relies on the imaginative capacity of the occupants to take full advantage of Thompson's inventive forms

Figure 106 The Children's School, Stamford, corridor from library to music/dining building

Structure, Skin, and Materials

Maryann Thompson conceives of architecture as a woven art form, a notion germane not only to her interest in integrating building and landscape but also to the manner in which she forges visual links between a building's structural members and its skin. Critical to her approach is the experience of a building and the spatial effects that derive from relationships between its structural systems and its material logics. She is inspired by the manner in which each might impart a psychological sense of stability, of calm, of relative enclosure or exposure, of physical comfort, or of wonder. These experiential qualities are furthered by the manner in which natural light serves as a medium to amplify visual relationships between structural and material systems.

Thompson associates her correlation between weaving and her mode of architectural expression with the theoretical formulations of Gottfried Semper. Her work, however, constitutes a significant departure from the hypothesis advanced by the nineteenth-century German architect and theorist. In *The Four Elements of Architecture* (1851), Semper associated textiles with his concept of the enclosure, not only in defining space, but also in a symbolic dimension, claiming "the carpet wall plays a most important role in the general history of art."[1] Semper noted that, as the earliest form of spatial enclosure, the woven carpet served to obscure the system of support and the mode of construction—aspects of MTA's architecture that she often strives to expose to view. For Thompson, a sense of a building's means of support, made visible through the interplay of structure and skin, can provide the occupant with a reassuring feeling of comfort and ease, while it contributes to the kinesthetic experience of space, just as the textures of natural materials appeal to the bodily sense of touch.

The manner in which the heavy timber framing in the **Straitsview Barn** on San Juan Island, Washington (Thompson and Rose, 1996-97), renders the structural logic of the system visible and comprehensible inspired Thompson to employ this traditional construction method—widely used in New England industrial and commercial buildings of the eighteenth and nineteenth centuries as well as barns—on several public projects. **[Fig. 107]**

For the **Visitor Center at the Polly Hill Arboretum** on Martha's Vineyard (Thompson and Rose/MTA, 1999–2001), she combined conventional heavy timber framing with contemporary construction techniques

1 Gottfried Semper, *The Four Elements of Architecture and Other Writings*, Harry Francis Malgrave and Wolfgang Hermann, trans. (Cambridge, UK and New York: Cambridge University Press, 1989), 103.

Figure 107 Straitsview Barn, San Juan Island, interior.

Figure 108 Visitor Center, Polly Hill Arboretum, West Tisbury, projecting facade segment

Figure 109
International School of Boston, upper school library

to create clear distinctions between structure and skin. This disparity is perceptible upon the approach to the building, where a glazed section of the facade is extended beyond a wooden corner column to accommodate a bench. [Fig. 108] The significance of this anomaly becomes clearer in the interior, where the freestanding corner column is clearly visible. Such independence of the structural members from the space-defining membranes of the walls, evident throughout the interior, is accentuated by the pronounced bulge at the midpoint of the columns—an expression of the compressive forces at play in the structure. Thompson's concern for consistent detailing extends to the information desk, where the horizontal and vertical elements are visibly distinct, and the recessed base makes the ensemble appear to float above the floor. [See Fig. 97]

During demolition for her renovation of the headquarters of the **International School of Boston** (2013–14), Thompson was delighted to discover heavy timber trusses in an existing turret, which became a prominent feature of the new upper school library. [Fig. 109]

Because heavy timber framing is compatible with the use of repurposed materials, she was able to conserve resources on both the residential and the farm structures at the **Slough Farm Foundation** on Martha's Vineyard (2015–18). In an overt reference to the vernacular origins of this type of construction, she used large wooden pegs to secure trusses or beams to columns whenever the means of connection among the heavy timber elements was exposed to view. [Fig. 110]

For the majority of her designs, which incorporate lighter supporting members, Thompson adapts the principle of structural expression inherent to heavy timber construction by drawing upon the aforementioned distinction between structure and skin. For example, the covered entry ramp at the **Atrium School** in Watertown (2005–06) reflects a didactic mode of expression in which galvanized steel structural supports

Figure 110 Slough Farm Foundation, Edgartown, yoga studio using traditiional heavy timber framing

Figure 111 Atrium School Watertown, entry ramp

Figure 112 Farm Life Center, Drumlin Farm, Concord, entrance canopy

contrast with the timber joists and wood decking of the soffit. [Fig. 111] The layered composition is reinforced by the treatment of the parapets, where infill panels of woven wire mesh are visually independent of their supporting members, which echo the galvanized steel columns of the ramp. Material disparities also contribute to the related effect of the canopy outside the **Farm Life Center at Drumlin Farm** in Lincoln (2008–11), where the polycarbonate sheathing that covers the Douglas fir purlins and beams enables natural light to permeate the entry threshold, reinforcing the visual independence of the systems. [Fig. 112]

Thompson's penchant for layering components of contrasting materials serves aesthetic and practical ends. At the **Science and Technology Center for The Foote School** in New Haven (2009–12), for example, external wooden louvered sunshades are visible

Figures 113 & 114
Jonathan Milikowsky Science and Technology Center, The Foote School, New Haven: trellis with solar thermal system; internal view of louvered windows

Figure 115 The Children's School, Stamford, classroom area with cross bracing

beyond the anodized aluminum window frames of a science classroom. As seen from the exterior, the louvers' horizontal pattern echoes the lines of the solar-thermal system in the wood-framed trellis below, imparting a decorative quality to these energy-saving devices. [Figs. 113 & 114]

To indicate that a wall is non-load bearing, Thompson occasionally positions windows directly below the relevant wall segment. More typically, she uses flush-framed windows in which the window header meets the supporting beam directly, without intervening framing. [See Figs. 12 & 13] In a related instance of structural expression, she enhances the open spatial qualities of her buildings by means of exposed steel cross bracing, which resolves the shear forces while obviating the need for cross walls to insure structural stability.

These methods are combined at **The Children's School** in Stamford (2003–07), where bookshelves at one end of the building are suspended from a pair of cross-braced steel columns. [Fig. 115] The structural logic of this ensemble is seen against a backdrop of flush-framed windows and external wooden louvers that impart a layered appearance to the whole. The woven effects of such examples derive from distinctions among the structural elements and enclosing skins and their material logics in which spatial stratification is primary.

The interweaving of elements is particularly evident in the detailing of the entrance lobbies for two of MTA's early educational facilities: the **Princeton University Child-care Center** (2013–18) and the **MGM Head Start and Family Center** in Springfield (2017–18). Cedar is used throughout the MGM lobby and adjoining corridor. [Fig. 116] The material uniformity underscores the im-

Figure 116 MGM Head Start and Family Center, Springfield, entrance lobby

Figure 117 Princeton University Child Care Center, Princeton, entrance lobby

pression of interweaving, which derives from the discrete articulation of each component—the framing of the panel beneath the flush-framed facade window, for example, or around the sliding window that opens to the office—and their collective aggregation. At Princeton, this effect is augmented by variations in materials, textures, and colors—from the dark cedar boards of the seating to the narrower tongue and groove cedar decking on the ceiling, the freestanding steel column, the mill finished anodized aluminum windows, and the zones of color in the linoleum flooring that distinguish spaces of circulation from those of repose. **[Fig. 117]**

The experiential value of Thompson's approach to architecture as a woven art form is particularly evident in the thickly layered thresholds that she uses to mediate the transition from exterior to interior. The modulation of structure and materials in these thresholds draws upon the kinesthetic sense of spatial dynamics accrued by the body in motion by introducing a momentary hiatus in the entry sequence in which the occupant is invited to pause, to reflect upon the capacity of architecture to affect the quality of day-to-day life within her buildings.

Nevertheless, Thompson does not embrace a rationalist approach to architectural expression. Indeed, in certain projects she provocatively aspires to impart a sense of wonder, to foment the viewer's curiosity by consciously manipulating the visual relationship between structure and skin. For example, the independence of these systems at the Polly Hill Visitor Center is accentuated by the misalignments between the beams and the skylight and between the exposed joint in the internal horizontal siding and the window jambs below. **[See Fig. 97]**

At the Walden Pond Visitor Center in Concord (2011–16), she achieved a related effect by selectively revealing aspects of the heavy timber structural system. Radiating beams in the form of an umbrella render the continuity of the roof visible above the internal walls of the public zone, which are capped by glazing to provide acoustic separation for the lecture space and the toilets. **[See Fig. 13]** The origin of the support system remains enigmatic, however, as the beams emanate from a point that is concealed behind the wooden cladding of the office walls, which extend to the ceiling. Through this material differentiation in the upper reaches of the volume, Thompson seeks to draw the viewer more fully into the moment of the architectural experience, to actively engage in the interpretation of the work.

Thompson frequently draws on variations in heavy timber framing. At the Leeper Studio Complex of the Atlantic Center for the Arts in New Smyrna Beach, Florida (Thompson and Rose, 1989–97), for example, she and Charles Rose used a variety of structural means, combining exposed heavy wooden trusses with concealed steel columns, light wood framing, and concrete bearing walls.**[See Fig. 126]** . At the Walden Pond Visitor Center, Thompson paired wooden columns with thin supports of tubular steel. **[See Figs. 12 & 72]** These hybrid systems enable her to minimize the dimensions of the structural timber and accentuate the lofty qualities of the respective spaces. Skylights placed above the wooden trusses in the painting studio and above the beams at the Visitor Center of the Polly Hill Arboretum amplify this relative sense of height and enable natural light to penetrate the respective structural zones, drawing attention to the independence of the systems—an idea Thompson accentuated at the Arboretum Visitor Center by displacing the skylight from the beams.

A similar phenomenon occurs in the open-air Leventritt Garden Pavilion at the Arnold Arboretum in Boston (Thompson and Rose/MTA, 1997–2002), where sunlight streaming through a gap between the angled roof planes heightens the contrast between the cedar joists and decking on the underside of the roof and the pavilion's supporting beams and columns of brushed steel, which appear luminous. **[See Figs. 5 & 135]** Thompson's

Figure 118 Smoketree House, Cambridge, columns composed of structural T-sections

Figure 119 The Oaks, Chilmark, living room column composed of structural T-sections with wooden posts held off the ground

interest in using natural light to heighten the juxtaposition of elements and materials in such examples is fundamental to her concept of architecture as a woven art form.

To amplify the apparent lightness of her columns, Thompson explores variations on this hybrid system of support. In numerous projects she fragments the column by substituting a pair of structural steel T-sections that are separated and joined at specific points (which vary according to the structural load) so that they operate as a single support. [Fig. 118] Elsewhere she combines a pair of structural steel T-sections with a wooden post that falls short of the floor plane. [Fig. 119] By distinguishing between the structural function of the steel and the aesthetic purpose of the wood, Thompson renders the dual role of the column explicit. In each case, the spatial effect is primary.

Further examples of ephemerality derive from Thompson's interest in capi-

Figure 120 H3 Biomedicine Lab (Esai Lab), Cambridge, corridor offices with translucent glass

talizing on the transparent and reflective capacities of glass at the **Eli and Edythe L. Broad Institute** in Cambridge (2004–06) and the **Early Learning Center for Novartis Pharmaceuticals Corporation** in East Rutherford, New Jersey (2012–15). Whereas the extensive use of glass partitions in the offices and laboratories of the Broad Institute was a means to further director Eric Lander's aspiration to promote an open and transparent process of scientific research, countering the isolation that he associates with the work of his peers, it challenged the scientists' need for a degree of privacy in their work lives. [See Fig. 26] For the offices of the **H3 Biomedicine Lab** in Cambridge (2010–11), Thompson addressed this issue by using translucent glass on the office partitions. [Fig. 120] In both examples, extensive glazing facilitates the presence of natural light throughout the depth of the building. In contrast, the internal glass partitions at the **Novartis Early Learning Center** can be interpreted as a positive means of surveillance, part of an effort to safeguard the children. More significant is the manner in which their reflective qualities serve to animate the circulation zone of ramps and collective spaces while furthering the visual interrelationship of interior and exterior. [See Fig. 56]

To draw upon the potential of light as a spatial medium, Thompson makes use of a light shelf—a horizontal ledge positioned below a strip of clerestory windows that draws upon a combination of natural and artificial sources of light to generate indirect lighting effects. [Fig. 121] At the top of the shelf, a fluorescent fixture or a strip of LED lighting is inset and covered with translucent Plexiglas so that the light source is concealed from view. The upper surface of the shelf is either finished in glossy paint or covered with mirrors to reflect the incoming natural light as well as that from the light fixture and project it onto the ceiling. As a result, the ceiling itself appears to be the light source. This effect, which amplifies the loftiness of a space, is further qualified at **The Oaks** on Martha's Vineyard (2007–13), where the shelf enables the dappled light that penetrates a zone of trees along the building perimeter to be projected onto the ceiling. By capitalizing upon the ephemeral quality of indirect lighting, Thompson prioritizes the spatial effects of light over the object quality of the light source in a manner that is analogous to the primacy she affords to the landscape setting over the object quality of her buildings.

Thompson's penchant for the extensive use of wood for walls and structural members in her projects derives from the reso-

Figure 121 Farm Life Center, Drumlin Farm, LIncoln, section diagram with light shelves

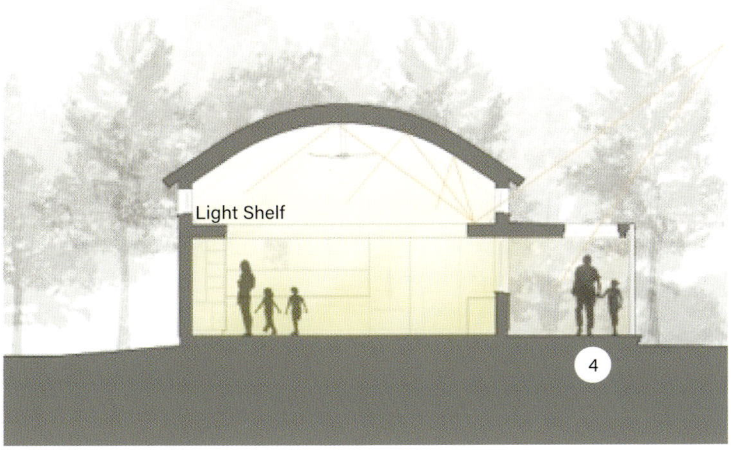

nance between the warmth of the human body and the thermal conductivity of wood, which contrasts with that of metal, glass, or stone, all of which draw heat out of the body through physical contact. The warmth of wood stems equally from its acoustic properties; its ability to dampen sound is an attribute that is particularly germane to her spaces of public assembly, such as the Great Room of the **Slough Farm Foundation** on Martha's Vineyard (2015–18). [Fig. 122]

In a related manner, Thompson's use of color is calculated to amplify the soothing psychological effects of her interiors. She is partial to tones found in nature—for example, the muted shades of green, brown, orange, and yellow velvet used on the seating of the **Rialto Restaurant and Bar** in Cambridge (2006–07), which were inspired by the variegated bark of nearby sycamore trees. [Fig. 123] For her educational interiors, she prefers the calming influence of such hues, contrary to the stimulating effect of bright colors preferred by many educators, such as those at the **MGM Head Start and Family Center**. [See Figs. 59–60, 66–67]

◆◆◆

Intrinsic to Thompson's notion of architecture as a woven art form is her passion for developing designs in which certain governing ideas prevail across a broad spectrum of scales, from the relationship between a building and its site to the details of the architectural casework. In making the constructional logic of her layered ensembles visible, she accords primacy to the spiritual, psychological, and emotional effects that emanate from the bodily experience of space. In a widely read essay from 1965, historian Eduard Sekler (Thompson's history professor at Harvard's Graduate School of Design and for whom she served as a teaching assistant), associates the visual effects of such material and structural assemblies with tectonics, as Shantel Blakely elaborates elsewhere in this volume.[2] [See pp. 66–75] In this sense, tectonics—the means by which structure and construction are raised to an art form—is an intrinsic aspect of Thompson's work.

2 Eduard Sekler, "Structure, Construction, Tectonics," in *Structure in Art and in Science*, György Kepes, ed. (New York: George Braziller, 1965), 89–95.

Figure 122 Slough Farm Foundation, Edgartown, Great Room viewed from mezzanine

Figure 123 Rialto Restaurant and Bar, Cambridge, bar seating.

Sustainability

Designing for sustainability—exploring architectural means to foster an equitable balance between human development and the Earth's biosphere—has been a guiding tenet for Maryann Thompson throughout her career. Through the extensive use of passive means of energy conservation, she seeks not only to limit the consumption of fossil fuels but also to foster cognizance of the ever-changing conditions of the natural environs. In accordance with her clients' particular requirements, moreover, these commonsense architectural methods, which derive from vernacular precedents, are often amplified by active means of energy conservation that stem from more recent technological advances.

Thompson's passive design strategies begin with site planning, in which she seeks to optimize the orientation of her buildings to the daily path of the sun and to the prevailing breezes. For the temperate climate of New England, she favors the use of large, south-facing, operable windows or sliding glass doors sheltered by overhangs, the depths of which are calculated to enable maximum solar exposure during the winter months, when the sun is relatively low in the sky, while protecting against direct solar penetration in the summer, when the sun is at a higher altitude. [Fig. 124]

Slab on grade construction provides thermal mass in which solar energy is absorbed during the daylight hours and radiated back in the evenings, thereby limiting the demand for mechanical heating. Cross

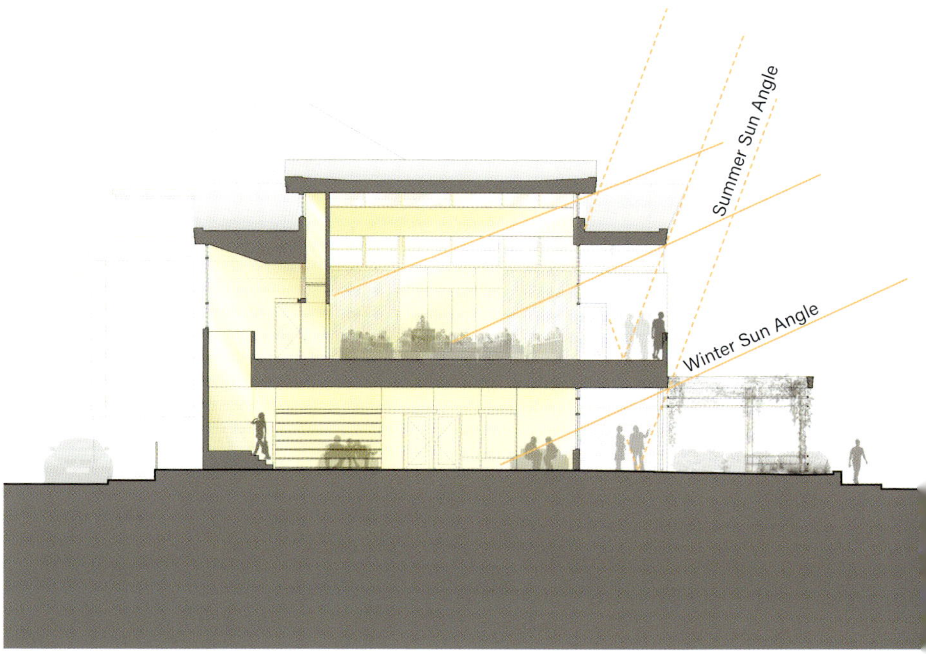

ventilation to reduce the reliance on air conditioning is facilitated by the stack effect, in which air entering through low windows is drawn out through clerestory windows or wind scoops in the upper reaches of a volume. Clerestory windows have the further benefit of drawing attention to the daily transit of the sun and to external weather conditions throughout a building's depth, reinforcing the interrelationship of interior and exterior and of ground and sky.

The use of solar radiation as an auxiliary heat source gained wide acceptance among modern architects practicing in New England in the late 1930s, as it not only afforded their designs a measure of economic efficiency but also drew upon the architectural principles of open space planning and the use of broad expanses of glass to visually link interior and exterior, as well as related means of expression grounded in regional climatic conditions.[1] During subsequent decades, however, when the supply of oil was both plentiful and relatively inexpensive, a reliance on mechanical means of heating and ventilating contributed significantly to the damaging environmental impact of what is now identified as climate change.

Cognizance of the increasing pace of this phenomenon and the associated sense of the planet's ecologic fragility has contributed to the broad interest among Thompson's clients in limiting their reliance on fossil fuels through passive means, while others have opted to supplement these methods with more recent technological methods for conserving natural resources. Although these technologies, which draw upon renewable energy sources—the sun, the wind, and geothermal energy—entail greater construction costs, they yield long-term advantages for both the client and the planet.

Thompson's interest in probing the design implications of such energy-saving methods stems from her undergraduate studies in architecture at Princeton, where faculty members Doug Kelbaugh and Harrison Fraker, along with Steve Slaby of the School of Engineering and Applied Sciences, were experimenting in innovative methods of solar heating. The essay she submitted with her Princeton application—on the threat posed by the earth's expanding ozone layer—is emblematic of her concern for the health of the planet. Mindful of the potential role of landscape design in this regard, Thompson earned professional degrees in both architecture and landscape architecture at Harvard's Graduate School of Design in 1989. Her studies focused on the interweaving of nature and people on the land, rather than on energy use.

An important influence was the courses she took with Harvard professor Richard Forman, who worked with colleagues from a range of disciplines to develop the foundations for the field of landscape ecology, synthesized in his book *Landscape Ecology* (1986). Forman's scientific studies of the gradated edge conditions found in nature had particular resonance for Thompson; she extrapolated the potential for such edge conditions to accommodate multiple habitats as having implications for the design of the interface between building and landscape. This insight would evolve into her penchant for conceiving of the facade as a layered membrane that moderates the transition from exterior to interior and works in conjunction with an overhanging roof to manage solar heat gain.

For her thesis—a water treatment plant in San Francisco—Thompson proposed a didactic spatial sequence in which the public would traverse the hilly site on a walkway that links a series of pavilions housing water treatment basins. These demonstrate the use of biological processes to convert wastewater to drinking water. She enlisted biologist John Todd, who was experimenting with ecological means to reposition such systems at the heart of public space, to serve as an external advisor on the project.[2]

A significant influence on Thompson's efforts to design in a sustainable manner is the work of mechanical engineer Marc Rosenbaum of Energysmiths (founded 1979). His expertise in passive house design

1 A number of architects associated with Harvard's Graduate School of Design were using passive solar means in their residential designs of the late 1930s; these include Walter Bogner, Marcel Breuer, Walter Gropius, G. Holmes Perkins, and Hugh Stubbins. See James Ford and Katherine Morrow Ford, *The Modern House in America* (New York: Architectural Book Publishing Co., 1940).

2 As a cofounder of the New Alchemy Institute in Falmouth, Massachusetts (1969–91) during the period when he was advising Thompson, John Todd was exploring ecologically sound ways of conceiving of and designing human support systems for food, water, and shelter. He founded his firm John Todd Ecological Design in 1988.

Figure 124 Temple Ahavat Achim, building section indicating solar angles of incidence

and net zero energy buildings, in which the total amount of energy used is equal to that produced on the site by renewable sources, led Thompson to request that Mass Audubon enlist him as a consultant on their Farm Life Center at Drumlin Farm in Lincoln (2008–11). Rosenbaum endorses an integrated systems approach to creating buildings and communities that connect humankind to the natural world and support personal and planetary health.[3] He is a certified member of the Passivhaus Institut, founded in Germany in 1996 to establish voluntary standards of energy efficiency. The institute's stringent guidelines include super insulated walls, slabs, and roofs, a limited amount of glazing from fixed triple-glazed windows, and a mechanical air exchange system that operates on electricity generated by solar energy.

To expand upon MTA's expertise in this area, Thompson took a course offered by the Passivhaus Institut in 2018. Wary of stringent adherence to methods that inhibit direct contact with the natural environs, however, she decided against becoming certified in the practice. In contrast to the lack of thermal breaks stipulated by the Passivhaus Institut requirements, Thompson prefers a hybrid heating and ventilation system that combines its mechanical air handling system, super-insulated walls, and triple-glazed windows with a permeable building envelope that incorporates extensive amounts of glass, with cross ventilation achieved by means of operable windows and boosted by ceiling fans. Recognizing the further potential for lowering energy consumption by heating the human body rather than the space, she hopes to develop a line of clothing that serves as a heat source, in effect providing a second skin between that of the body and that of the building.

During the late 1990s, concern for the adverse environmental effects of the building industry led the U.S. Green Building Council to develop its LEED (Leadership in Energy and Environmental Design) rating system to measure environmental performance from a whole building standpoint, as projected over a structure's life cycle.[4] In the early decades of the twenty-first century, as the sustainability movement became more widespread, the Living Future Institute was established as an international force for change, with the aim of fostering regenerative design. Going above and beyond the LEED certification standards, the Living Future Institute stipulates that buildings must be net-zero or net-positive energy use and free of toxic chemicals. While numerous MTA projects are LEED certified, only the MGM Head Start and Family Center in Springfield (2017–18) meets the more stringent criteria established by the Living Future Institute. [Fig. 125] The trajectory of Thompson's sustainability efforts is indicative of her clients' increasing attention to the environmental impact of their commissions.

Figure 125 MGM Head Start and Family Center, Springfield

The need to address the harsh conditions of the subtropical southern Florida climate at the Leeper Studio Complex of the Atlantic Center for the Arts in New Smyrna Beach, Florida (1989–97) brought issues of designing for sustainability to the fore. This commission, contracted while Thomp-

3 See Marc Rosenbaum biography at energysmiths.com.

4 In 2020 the Green Building Council introduced Net Zero LEED certification to indicate that a building is highly energy efficient and fully powered from on-site and/or off-site renewable energy sources. LEED criteria include credits for the use of non-toxic materials, sustainably harvested materials, local materials, and recycled and reclaimed materials.

Figure 126 Leeper Studio Complex, Atlantic Center for the Arts, New Smyrna Beach, sectional model through painting studio with wind scoops

son and Charles Rose were working in the office of landscape architect Michael Van Valkenburgh, prompted the pair to launch their independent practice two years later. Thompson and Rose used various means to mediate the region's intense heat, sun, and humidity in their complex of pavilions, which they carefully attuned to the densely vegetated site. Expansive walls of glass maximize northern light, external wooden louvers lessen the effects of direct sunlight on the interiors, roof overhangs minimize solar heat gain, and light monitors inspired by North-African wind scoops draw upon the stack effect for ventilation. **[Fig. 126]**

Certain MTA clients seek to supplement such passive means of energy conservation with active technological means, such as solar thermal collectors, photovoltaic arrays, and geothermal systems.[5] Notable early examples include two residences carried out during the early years of Thompson's independent practice: the **Geothermal House** in Belmont (2001–03) and the **Zero Impact House** in North Easton (2004–06).

Thompson's experience with active methods of energy conservation began with the **Geothermal House**. The decision to incorporate a geothermal system to satisfy the project's heating and cooling requirements emerged only gradually over the course of her conversations with the clients, who initially sought to limit the environmental impact of their residence through passive means alone. To facilitate access to natural light and cross ventilation, Thompson distributed the program requirements in three wings that are angled to form a north-facing entry court. Relatively closed facades facing the court contrast with large sliding glass doors in the principal volumes that open fully to the site. Cross ventilation in the south-facing living room is supplemented by operable clerestory windows. A large outdoor sitting area framed by overhanging trellises admits dappled light to the principal volumes in summer, while opening them fully to the winter sun. **[Fig. 127]** These passive means of energy conservation are supplemented by the geothermal system, in which a closed-loop array of liquid-filled tubes is inserted into wells that penetrate five hundred feet into the bedrock to take advantage of the earth's constant temperature of fifty

5 In solar thermal technology, a non-freezing fluid in a closed loop is heated by the sun and drawn through a heat exchanger, which transfers the heat to the building's domestic hot water system. In contrast, photovoltaic arrays use semiconductors to generate electricity for heating and cooling directly. The latter system only works when the sun is out, so that its output is affected on a cloudy day, but the excess energy can be sold back to the utility company, generating income.

Figure 127 Geothermal House, Belmont, terrace with trellis

to sixty degrees Fahrenheit. The mechanics of the system are concealed in the basement, where a heat pump transfers energy from the tubes to supply the house's heating and cooling requirements.

Energy conservation was a priority from the outset of MTA's commission to design the **Zero Impact House**, whose clients were familiar with the Geothermal House. The first residence in Massachusetts to achieve LEED silver certification, this compact, all-electric house incorporates rooftop photovoltaic panels to meet its energy requirements, resulting in no greenhouse gas emissions—all accomplished within a limited budget. [Fig. 128] To optimize southern exposure, a large clearing was created on the wooded site, and the house was sited near its northern edge. During the winter, a thick concrete slab-on-grade operates as a thermal mass to absorb solar heat through the extensive fenestration on the south-facing entry facade, which is supplemented by two pellet stoves. The radiant heat from the stove pipes is sufficient to heat the second floor, while the super-insulated skin and thermally efficient windows enable surplus

Figure 128 Zero Impact House, North Easton, south-facing entry facade

Figure 129 Farm Life Center, Drumlin Farm, Lincoln

energy generated by the photovoltaic system to be sold back to the local supplier. In the summer, a roof overhang works with the canopy of deciduous trees, introduced to shield the south-facing windows from direct solar exposure. Recycled and energy-efficient materials include a rubber roofing system made from used tires, reclaimed hardwood carpentry, casework, and flooring, and recycled bathroom tiles.

Several commissions in the public domain provided further opportunities for Thompson to experiment with the possibilities of net zero design. To conform to its environmental ethic, Mass Audubon engaged Marc Rosenbaum to work as a consultant on the design of Thompson's **Farm Life Center**, which serves as the visitor center for its facility at **Drumlin Farm** in Lincoln. With the exception of its operable windows, the design adheres generally to Passivhaus Institut guidelines. The high-performance building envelope includes triple-glazed windows, twelve-inch-thick walls, and ultra-tight construction. [Fig. 129] The south-facing windows surmounted by light shelves and clerestory windows work together with skylights to satisfy lighting needs until late afternoon, while the curved ceiling facilitates its even distribution. [See Fig. 121] Other sustainable elements include the use of site-milled lumber for siding, a state-of-the-art mechanical system with energy recovery, and dedicated solar arrays placed atop a new goat shed and an existing sheep shelter. The net zero energy building is certified LEED gold by the U.S. Green Building Council. Thompson subsequently enlisted Rosenbaum to work with her on the **Egret Meadow House** on Martha's Vineyard (2011–14), and the insights that he brought to these two projects would continue to influence her design process.

In keeping with the environmental values associated with the legacy of Henry David Thoreau, the **Walden Pond Visitor Center** in Concord (2011–16) is also an all-electric, net zero building that similarly draws upon Passivhaus principles. While its triple-paned windows and super insulated walls conserve heat during the winter, ample operable windows and ceiling fans facilitate a reliance on natural light and ventilation during the warmer months, when only the offices are air conditioned. A large photovoltaic array in the parking lot provides shade for the automobiles while fully supplying the building's energy needs. [Fig. 130] The conservation of resources was also a motivating factor in the selection of building materials. Although the Visitor Center's primary structural members are Douglas fir, its interior walls and flooring are composed of locally sourced wood. The exterior siding and decking is heat-treated as a preservative, and wood salvaged from trees cut down during construction was used to construct the interior furniture and fittings.

Figure 130 Walden Pond Visitor Center, Concord, parking under photovoltaic arrays

Exceeding the energy-saving tactics found in Thompson's other educational designs, the MGM Head Start and Family Life Center includes a super-insulated building envelope, triple-glazed windows, a geothermal system for heating and cooling, and a rooftop photovoltaic system. [See Fig. 125] Cross ventilation afforded by the operable windows is supplemented by ceiling fans. Further energy efficient features include LED lighting regulated by occupancy and daylight sensors, point-of-use water heaters, and low-flow plumbing fixtures, with all devices controlled by an automated building management system. Because the building's energy requirements are supplied by the photovoltaic system, it not only achieved LEED platinum certification but also fulfilled the stringent guidelines for Zero Energy certification from the International Living Future Institute.

The didactic value of making such active means of energy conservation palpable to observers—a significant feature of Thompson's Harvard thesis—is a strategic aspect of both the Farm Life Center at Drumlin Farm and the Walden Pond Visitor Center, where the solar arrays are visually conspicuous. The educational potential of such methods is also germane to the Jonathan Milikowsky Science and Technology Center for The Foote School in New Haven (2009–12), where the photovoltaic array is confined to south-facing roof surfaces, and hence out of sight, while the significant role of a louvered trellis that diffuses daylight entering the western classrooms is not visually evident. [See Fig. 113] It incorporates a solar thermal system that provides all of the building's hot water. Further energy-saving measures include a super-insulated skin, operable windows set high in the walls to facilitate cross ventilation, and a reliance on daylighting through large expanses of glass that are shielded by roof overhangs. To render the effects of this combination of active and passive methods of energy conservation palpable, a system in the entrance lobby that tracks the building's hot water and energy production and use in conjunction with weather data can be used for lessons in environmental sustainability.

In many of Thompson's projects, resource conservation is facilitated through the use of reclaimed materials. At The Foote School, wood salvaged from the former seats of the renovated Yale Bowl was used for benches and countertops, while the stair treads and casework were fabricated from white oak repurposed from an Amish barn in Pennsylvania. Other exam-

Figure 131 Pier 6 Warming Hut, Brooklyn Bridge Park, Brooklyn, NY

Figure 132 Visitor Center, Stevens-Coolidge House and Gardens, North Andover

Figure 133 Slough Farm Foundation, Edgartown, corn crib seating area

ples include the Warming Hut at Brooklyn Bridge Park (2006–11), where Thompson wrapped the external ramp in a skin of spaced longleaf pine timbers reclaimed from a nearby structure that the New York City Parks Department had slated for demolition. [Fig. 131] For the benches outside the Walden Pond Visitor Center, Michael Van Valkenburgh used live oak slabs that had been preserved in underwater storage tanks at the Charlestown Navy Yard since the 1600s, when they were imported for repairing frigates.

The reuse of existing structures is another prominent feature of Thompson's work. Examples include the warehouse in Watertown that was revamped for the Atrium School in Watertown (2005–06) and the maintenance shed at the Stevens-Coolidge House and Gardens in North Andover that was transformed to serve as a Visitor Center for the Trustee of Reservations property (2019–21). [Fig. 131] At Slough Farm on Martha's Vineyard (2015–18), where the structural system incorporates reclaimed heavy timbers, the galvanized steel frame of an old corn crib was repurposed to support vines sheltering an outdoor seating area, while the existing silo, restored for potential use as an observatory, serves as a beacon for the site. [Fig. 133; see Fig. 17]

◆◆◆

The use of recycled construction materials and structures operates together with Thompson's widespread use of active and/or passive means of energy conservation to limit the ecological footprint of the work. Her experience in designing for energy conservation has led Thompson to favor all-electric solutions, with energy supplied by solar thermal systems. She anticipates that the potential for ongoing technological improvements, greater affordability of related technologies, and increased public understanding of the causes and consequences of climate change will contribute in significant ways to her practice in the coming years.

Figure 134 Overleaf Leventritt Garden Pavilion, Arnold Arboretum, Boston

Part III
Projects

Civic and Cultural Institutions

In her public commissions for nonprofit arts, religious, and civic organizations, as well as those for private institutions devoted to scientific research, Maryann Thompson explores various architectural means to foster communal engagement and human interaction. This theme is particularly germane to an early project that Thompson undertook in partnership with Charles Rose—the **Leeper Studio Complex at the Atlantic Center for the Arts** in New Smyrna Beach, Florida (1989–97). To accommodate a residency program for writers, dancers, visual artists, composers, choreographers, and artists, the complex includes a black box theater, painting and sculpture studios, a recording studio, a dance studio, a library, and various support spaces.

The interdisciplinary nature of the organization led Thompson and Rose to distribute these programmatic elements across an enclave of seven pavilions, linked together by a boardwalk that threads through the site's dense subtropical vegetation. [Figs. 135–36] The complex is never fully grasped as a whole owing to the fragmented experience of its unfolding spatial sequence. Moreover, the buildings are never revealed as distinct objects. Instead, segments of their discrete volumes are seen from a set of clearings created in the dense undergrowth by widened sections of the boardwalk that are fitted with benches. Although the need to foster interdisciplinary exchange among the residents might suggest a more cohesive approach to the building program, this dispersal affords a measure of seclusion for the individual artists, while it incorporates specific spaces for collaboration in the clearings and the performance spaces. Moreover, the labyrinthine experience of the sequence prompts creative exploration of the complex, facilitating modes of collaboration that could never be scripted in spatial terms.

After founding her independent practice in 2000, Thompson continued to challenge conventional architectural means of encouraging the cross fertilization of ideas. The 2004 commission from the American Repertory Theater (A.R.T.) to develop the black box **Zero Arrow Theater** in Cambridge (2004–06, no longer extant) provided a vehicle for her to expand upon this theme.[1] Artistic director Robert Woodruff conceived of the space as a satellite to the A.R.T. facilities in Harvard's Loeb Drama Center (1958–59), designed by Hugh Stubbins, where the innovative theater consultant George Izenour created the first black box theater in the United States. In Stubbins' and Izenour's design,

1 Founded in New Haven as the Yale Repertory Theater in 1966, the American Repertory Theater moved to Harvard's Loeb Drama Center in 1980, where it continues to operate.

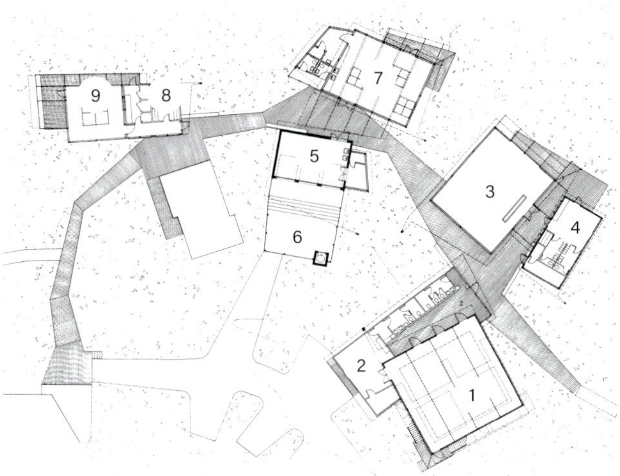

Figures 135 & 136 Leeper Studio Complex, Atlantic Center for the Arts, New Smyrna Beach: view from secondary approach; site plan

1. Black Box Theater
2. Gallery / Reception
3. Dance Studio
4. Dressing Room
5. Sculpture Studio
6. Outdoor Sculpture Yard
7. Painting Studio
8. Audio Room
9. Music Room

students were able to launch productions without faculty supervision, no admission was charged, and overflow audiences quickly became the norm. This type of unadorned performance space, with a flat floor that can be adapted to fit the staging and seating requirements of different types of theatrical production, quickly became the norm, as exemplified by the black box theater that Thompson and Rose designed at the Atlantic Center for the Arts.

In the spirit of innovation that inspired its predecessor, Woodruff envisioned Harvard's Zero Arrow Theater as an incubator for new work, with different theatrical productions offered each night. Thompson positioned the lobby/exhibition space so that it adjoins a tree-lined, mid-block

Figures 137 & 138
Zero Arrow Theater, Cambridge: lobby; interior set up as Oberon nightclub/ theater

alley, where it might arouse the curiosity of passersby. [Fig. 137] With temporary exhibitions devised to provoke discussion among audience members, the brightly lit lobby contrasts with the darkened environment of the theater, where the actions of the performers and their interaction with the audience are foregrounded. Thompson supplemented the conventional form of the black box theater with an overhead catwalk system. Originally intended to support adjustable lighting and sound equipment, it inspired directors to extend the possibilities for performance to the upper reaches of the volume.

Although Woodruff's period of experimentation was short lived, the transformation envisioned six years later by his successor, Diane Paulus, was achieved primarily through changes in how the space is equipped and used, rather than through any architectural modifications. As part of her ambition to have a greater influence on cultural production in the United States, Paulus conceived of the venue as a vehicle for emerging artists to imagine new projects that could only exist in such diverse environments as a simple platform or the more elaborate form of a club/theater. Through the addition of disco lights, a fully-stocked bar, and implementation of a liberal cell phone policy, for example, the Zero Arrow Theater was transmuted for an early Paulus production into the Oberon, a nightclub/theater fostering a fully interactive theatrical experience. [Fig. 138]

In her work for a variety of religious organizations, Thompson has focused largely on the communal aspirations of each institution. With her modest addition to the interdenominational **First Parish Church** of Lincoln, Massachusetts (2013–18), for example, she reorganized the annex at the rear of the historic Greek Revival sanctuary to create a generous reception space, which is accessed from a covered porch, equipped with an adjoining pantry/kitchen, and opens directly to a patio that overlooks the rear garden. [Fig. 139] To maintain the dominance of the sanctuary, she gave her addition a low profile and detailed its white, wood-framed exterior in a traditional manner consistent with the aesthetic of the historic Protestant churches that face onto New England village greens. This means of symbolizing communal values via the aesthetic of the historic edifice contrasts with that on the interior, where Thompson relied on natural wood finishes to impart a warm, welcoming atmosphere.

While this project was underway, Claire Feingold Thoryn, the minister of the First Parish Church in Lincoln, moved to the **Follen Community Church** in Lexington (1840), where she enlisted MTA to renovate an annex that had been built in the 1990s to house social spaces and classrooms. The annex sits atop a one-story base designed by Sally Harkness, a congregation member and partner in The Architects Collaborative.

The original nineteenth-century structure was conceived of by its minister, Charles Follen, as a "Free" Christian church, open to all.[2] Trained in architecture in his native Germany, Follen envisioned the hexagonal form of the sanctuary as a means to foster a more intimate relationship with his parishioners. Seeking to have members of the congregation play active roles in the services, he intended to preach at the level of the floor rather than from a pulpit, and he viewed the status of women as equal to that of men.

2 Charles Follen was appointed minister to the Lexington congregation in 1849, but he died in a fire before the building was dedicated in January 1840. See Anne Grady and Walter Leutz, "Charles Follen, the East Village, and Abolitionism" (2017), https://follen.org/wp-content/uploads/2017/10/Charles-Follen-the-East-Village-and-Abolitionism.pdf

Figure 139 First Parish Church of Lincoln, pedestrian route to annex entry

Figures 140–142
Follen Community Church, Lincoln: view toward new entry court; annex stair; music room

With her modifications of 2017 to 2020, Thompson sought to imbue the annex with the egalitarian, communal ethos of Follen's design by reconfiguring the means of access and carrying out extensive renovations to the interior. These extend well beyond simple compliance with the accessibility requirements of the Americans with Disabilities Act of 1990, a civil rights law that prohibits discrimination based on disability. A new entry sequence leads from Massachusetts Avenue up a shallow ramp to a paved courtyard bounded by a covered walkway. **[Fig. 140]** The walkway links the classroom spaces in an adjoining house with a new lobby behind the sanctuary; its open stair and elevator lead to the various levels of the annex. **[Fig. 141]** The sequence culminates in a lofty music room on the uppermost floor, where an adjoining kitchen enables it to be used for receptions as well as performances. **[Fig. 142]** To improve access to the side entrance of Harkness' addition, used for entry to classrooms and a large meeting room, Thompson added a ramp and fronted it with a covered porch.

For the **Congregation B'nai Israel** in Northampton (2018, 2021–), Thompson proposed a renovation and addition to the group's existing synagogue in which she explored variations on ideas that she had realized in the Temple Ahavat Achim in Gloucester (2009–12). In an early schematic design, a generous new lobby leads directly

Figures 143 & 144
Congregation B'nai Israel, Northampton: ground floor plan; perspective of entry patio

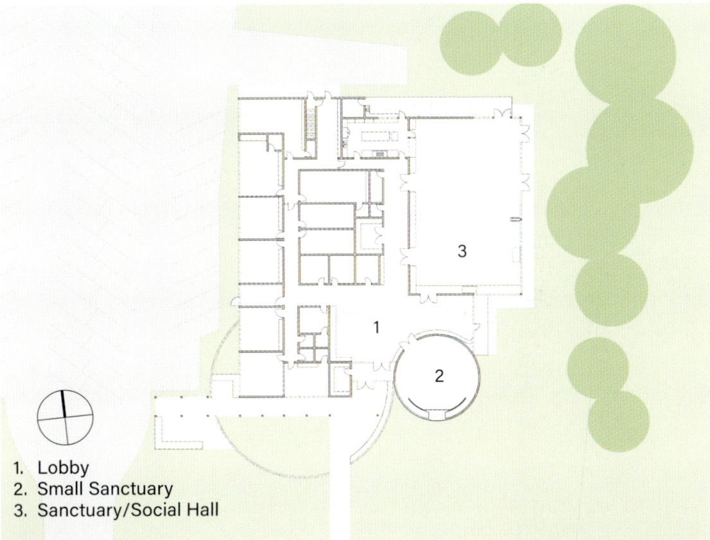

to both a small chapel and a larger combination social hall and sanctuary, which opens to an existing prayer garden. [Fig. 143] In front of the building, Thompson developed three patios, each lined with benches. The largest, directly in front of the entry, is fully open to view, while a perforated brick wall affords a measure of privacy for the two smaller patios, which are reached by a covered walkway. [Fig. 144] The lobby is also fitted with sitting areas of various sizes, providing further opportunities for casual social encounters. To accommodate the different congregation sizes for regular weekly services versus those on the High Holy Days, Thompson subdivided the existing sanctuary and used its original semicircular apse to create a new, smaller chapel, which can alternately be used as a study or meeting space. Illumination from a strip of clerestory windows contrasts with the indirect lighting that penetrates the layers of the perforated brick facade and wooden screens to either side of the Torah ark, which is built into the wall. The remaining part of the original sanctuary, like the larger volume in the Temple Ahavat Achim, can accommodate dinners or community meetings as well as religious services. Although both ritual spaces in the Congregation B'nai Israel are designed to accommodate flexible uses, their spiritual qualities are achieved in different ways—through the varied qualities of light in the smaller chapel and direct exposure to the natural elements of the prayer garden in the larger volume.

Two civic projects for which Thompson developed schematic designs—the **Lincoln Community Center** (2017–18, 2022) and the **Vineyard Haven Public Library** (2019, 2024–)—similarly exemplify her propensity for drawing upon and amplifying the qualities of a site. In Lincoln, Thompson configured her Community Center to the north of the Hartwell Elementary School, near an adjoining middle school, so that the entire complex would be dominated by landscape. Relocating an existing parking lot enabled her to propose a new open space—the Hartwell Green—east of the middle school playing fields, thereby improving the condition of the intervening wetlands and linking these major green spaces by walkways. [See

Figure 145 Vineyard Haven Public Library addition, perspective

[Fig. 87] The Center, which is to serve local community organizations as well as the Council on Aging, contains a programmatic amalgam: art and sound studios, meeting spaces, and a fitness center, all overlooking the Hartwell Green. The project's communal aspirations are evident not only in its verdant new landscape but also in the building's more intimate spaces for casual gathering. Thompson conceived of the corridor as a nexus of activity where the paths of the users would overlap as they move from one program to the next. She varied its dimensions and provided seating to foster spontaneous encounters among the town's senior citizens.

In MTA's addition to the **Vineyard Haven Public Library**, Thompson sought to forge a more direct relationship between interior and exterior by opening the principal library level to a new garden that adjoins the lofty open volume of the new wing. When completed, it will accommodate lectures, community meetings, and yoga classes. [Fig. 145] A second garden will replace the existing concrete pad that adjoins the basement level stacks, where the children's library will be relocated.

The challenge to foster impromptu encounters among staff members of nonprofit organizations devoted to scientific research inspired three MTA projects in Kendall Square, an area adjacent to the MIT campus that was being redeveloped into a hub of biotechnology research. These transformations began in 2003, when Thompson was commissioned to renovate a zone of offices and meeting spaces at the **Whitehead Institute for Biomedical Research** (2003–04), an offshoot of MIT dedicated to improving human health. Institute director Eric Lander was well acquainted with Thompson's working method, as she had previously renovated an existing building to serve as his family's principal residence. With this new renovation, Lander sought to challenge conventional approaches to scientific research by encouraging more active dialogue among scientists, whose typical comportment he viewed as hermetic. In response, Thompson distributed the scientists' offices around an open central area, which she equipped with a small kitchen, a serving bar, and groupings of comfortable seating arrayed beneath skylights, so that natural light permeates the entire volume. [Fig. 146] To reiterate the integral relationship between this central zone and the offices, which are open to view through glazed partitions, she devised a sinuous pattern in the carpeting. Subtle shifts in the carpet's colors transgress any sense of boundary between the zones. Despite the extreme modesty of this design, the architectural means that Thompson devised to encourage the exchange of ideas and the collective use of space would have repercussions for her next, more substantial commission from Lander—a new building for the **Eli and Edythe L. Broad Institute** (2004–06), of which he was founding director.

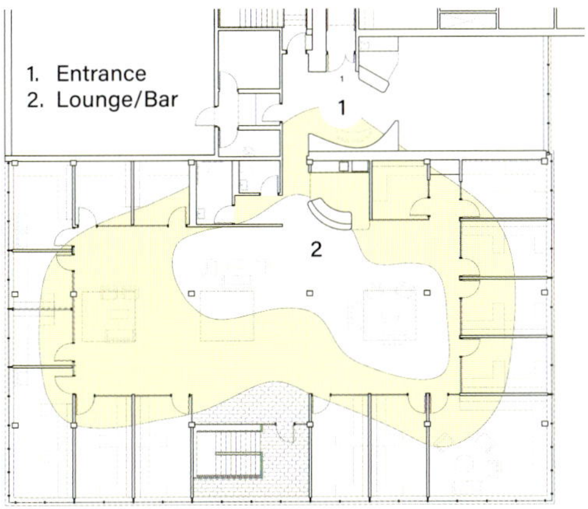

Figure 146 Whitehead Institute for Biomedical Research, Cambridge, plan

At the Broad Institute, Lander encouraged Thompson to devise further means to facilitate an open, collaborative approach to scientific research. In addition to providing a protracted entry sequence in which scientists might engage with the public as well as converse among themselves, Thompson equipped each of the building's seven upper levels with a kitchenette, a bar, and a comfortable seating area, along with Lander's concept of a casual "sock path" that threads through the glass-enclosed laboratories and office spaces—all intended to foster impromptu encounters among Institute members and their associates from diverse scientific fields. [See Figs. 25–27]

The extreme transparency of this spatial sequence is challenged in Thompson's third medical research facility in the vicinity of Kendall Square, the **H3 Biomedicine Lab** (2010–11). This oncology research laboratory, a subsidiary of the Tokyo based pharmaceuticals company Eisai Co., Ltd., was co-founded by Tod Golub, a pioneer in the field of cancer genomics who was affiliated with both the Whitehead Institute and the Broad Institute, where he served on the design committee and directed the program in cancer research (2004–21) before being named director. (Golub had also enlisted Thompson to design a private residence—in this case a vacation house in Western Massachusetts.) In 2011, he commissioned MTA to transform one floor of an existing office building into laboratory and workspaces for the company's new headquarters in Technology Square—a 1960s-era development designed by Eduardo Catalano that was undergoing extensive renovation as part of MIT's effort to advance new vehicles for research into biotechnology and information technology.

Thompson subdivided the space into three general areas: a zone of offices and meeting spaces that links the laboratories devoted to chemistry and biology, respectively. In a variation of her layout for the Broad Institute, she dispersed a reception area, open zones of cubicles for the office staff, conference rooms, and an informal sitting area equipped with a bar/kitchenette along a corridor that winds through the offices and meeting rooms. [Fig. 147] To encourage the informal exchange of ideas and facilitate wayfinding amid the repetitive offices and subsidiary spaces, she curved the principal circulation route and varied the forms of these collective spaces. In response to Golub's request to afford the scientists greater privacy than had been the case at the Broad Institute, she combined translucent and transparent glazing on the walls of the offices that line the corridor, restricting transparency to their lower and upper zones to provide privacy while enabling natural light to permeate the entire sequence. [Fig. 148]

◆◆◆

Thompson's work in the public domain—whether directed to creative, spiritual, or civic ends or to public good in the form of medical research—reflects the value she places on architecture as a means of promoting human exchange and its potential to foster a communal ambiance. Her forays into these themes reflect contrasting design approaches. These include exploiting the tension between isolation and collaboration to instigate creativity at the Atlantic Center for the Arts while attempting to mitigate the self-imposed isolation of scientists in institutions devoted to research, or creating a neutral platform to foster direct interaction of audience and performers at the Zero Arrow Theater versus conceiving of architecture as an active agent in promoting social encounters in her various civic commissions.

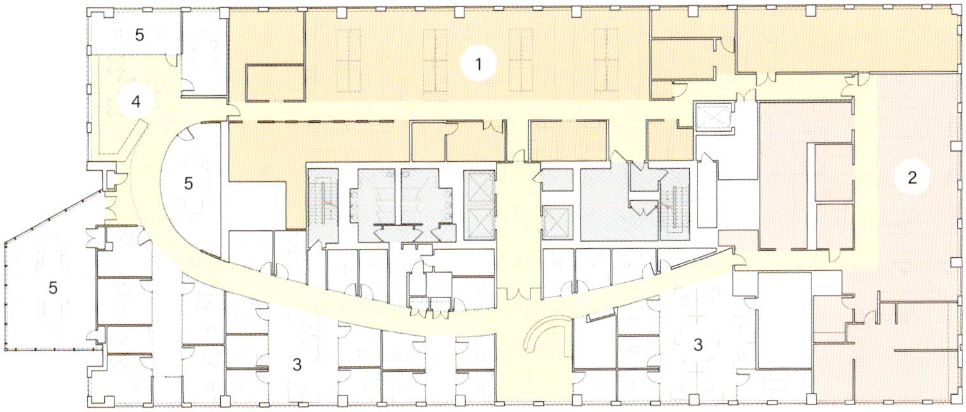

1. Chemistry
2. Biology
3. Offices
4. Lounge/Bar
5. Conference

Figures 147 & 148
H3 Biomedicine Lab, Cambridge: plan; view to lounge/bar

Park Pavilions and Visitor Centers

A significant body of Thompson's creative output consists of visitor centers and recreational pavilions for public parks and gardens. Several of these projects are components of large open sites, while others are more constrained by their contexts or involve the adaptive reuse of existing structures. In each case, the design was driven by an underlying social motivation. To prompt broad public use of the amenities offered by these sites, Thompson devised spatial sequences to guide the visitors in their experiences of these landscapes.

A trio of Thompson and Rose projects, for which Thompson took primary responsibility, provided diverse opportunities to build upon her interest in the interrelationship of architecture and landscape. For the **Bathhouse and Amphitheater at NARA Park** in North Acton (Thompson and Rose, 1998–2000), she explored the potential for architecture to create an experiential sequence that engages relationships among the elements of a landscape. With the open-air classroom at the **Leventritt Garden of the Arnold Arboretum** in Boston (Thompson and Rose/MTA, 1997–2002), completed after she established her independent practice, Thompson worked with landscape architects Reed Hilderbrand to elaborate upon this theme, while conceiving of her design in terms of a dialogue between forms of human manufacture and those of natural origin. Similar ideas also prevailed at the **Visitor Center at the Polly Hill Arboretum** on Martha's Vineyard (Thompson and Rose/MTA, 1999–2001), where Thompson drew upon her principle of sublimating her architecture to the exigencies of the site to develop passive means of energy conservation derived from vernacular design traditions—an approach that would have enduring significance for her architecture.
[See pp. 13–18]

The commission from the Acton Recreation Center to design a new bathhouse and concert venue at **NARA Park** provided an opportunity for Thompson to experiment with the integration of architecture and landscape at a new scale. The project was part of a larger effort to augment the town's recreational facilities by transforming the forty-acre site of a former gravel pit into a general recreational area. The project includes a swimming pond, bathhouse, amphitheater, and associated parking lots and infrastructure.

Thompson worked with the project manager Tom Tidman, NARA Park's natural resources director, to position the bathhouse and amphitheater in an experiential sequence relative to the amenities laid out by

1 The Nathan Allen Recreational Area Park in North Acton is known as NARA Park.

Figures 149 & 150
Bathhouse and Amphitheater, NARA Park, North Action: entry pavilion breezeway framing view to amphitheater; stage

his team of engineers and construction workers. She positioned a combination entry pavilion and bathhouse so that the breezeway between its two components frames the open-air amphitheater and covered stage, visible in the distance. [Fig. 149] To the right of the breezeway, a ticket office and a large, covered deck for outdoor dining overlook a man-made beach and the swimming pond, which was excavated from the former quarry. To the left are the toilets and changing cubicles—with the latter open to the elements. Both the entry pavilion and bathhouse are covered by single gabled roof. Atop the breezeway, a U-shaped void is excised from the roof to frame the sky, a visual impression that contrasts with the haptic experience of the exposed aggregate embedded in the pavilion's concrete floor, which was sourced from the quarry.

A related grounded quality characterizes the grass-covered amphitheater, where fill excavated from the pond was used to build up the semicircular landform at its edge. This contrasts with the buoyant quality of the stage—a simple shed roof that appears to float on triangulated steel columns above a wooden deck. [Fig. 150] The backstage area is defined by an irregular line of simple wooden fencing, while wiring embedded in the mound and in the columns is used to power portable lighting elements and speakers for use during concerts or occasional theatrical performances.

Several of Thompson's designs for park pavilions and visitor centers were inspired by the historic legacies of their sites. For example, the circulation system and spatial patterns of the Arnold Arboretum as originally laid out by Frederick Law Olmsted in-

Figures 151 & 152
Polly Hill Arboretum, West Tisbury: south-facing terrace; the Bower created by Polly Hill

spired Thompson to devise the vine trellises and open-air **Leventritt Garden Pavilion** to form an unfolding sequence of framed views toward the garden terraces designed by Reed Hilderbrand. [See Figs. 3 & 4] The historic farm and woodland of the **Polly Hill Arboretum**, which traces its origins to the island's early settlers, inspired Thompson to situate her **Visitor Center** and toilet pavilion so that they minimally impinge upon the arboretum landscape. Hill's shady retreat, the Bower, was a precedent for the trellises made from black locust boughs that Thompson used to frame the courtyard linking the two structures. [Figs. 151 & 152] In deference to the area where Henry David Thoreau spent over two years living in his cabin, she positioned her **Walden Pond Visitor Center** in Concord (2011–16) so that the entry sequence would focus on the pond, rather than on the new building. [See Fig. 80] Finally, for her pavilion at **Charlesbank Landing** on the Boston Esplanade (2017–18, 2023–), Thompson paid tribute to the area's historical affiliation with Olmsted's Charlesbank proposal of 1892, which was developed during the early 1900s as the first outdoor gymnasium in the United States. She provided a ramp to a roof deck viewing platform that overlooks the adjoining basketball courts and baseball fields, as well as boating events on the Charles River. [See Figs. 20 & 21]

Thompson created many of her park projects with her frequent collaborator Michael Van Valkenburgh. These include the aforementioned **Visitor Center at the Polly Hill Arboretum**, where he sought to minimize the effects of the new construction on the site, and at **Walden Pond**, where he used native trees and shrubs to emulate the qualities of the existing landscape. In contrast, for the brownfield site at **Corktown Common** in Toronto (2006–11), Van Valkenburgh devised a flood-mitigation infrastructural system that combines a low-lying prairie with a massive landform inspired by the native landscapes of Ontario. Thompson's pavilion rises above a wooded knoll at the top of the hill, where it serves as an orientation device within the park. [See Fig. 22]

Thompson also worked with Van Valkenburgh on two adaptive reuse proj-

Figure 153 Pier 2 Recreational Center, Brooklyn Bridge Park (with MVVA)

ects that are components of his **Brooklyn Bridge Park** in Brooklyn, New York. For a new sport and recreational hub at **Pier 2** (2006–14), she selectively demolished parts of the existing four-acre warehouse to create open-air zones for basketball and shuffleboard. She inserted skylights in the warehouse's corrugated metal gable roofs to augment daylighting for the covered sports facilities and demolished the existing facades to enhance natural ventilation and afford views across the East River to lower Manhattan. [Fig. 153]

Thompson's coeval adaptive reuse project involved transforming a mechanical building at the head of Pier 6 into a **Warming Hut** (2006–11) to facilitate year-round use of the park. Situated at a major pedestrian access point from Atlantic Avenue, it houses an information office, public restrooms, and a café with indoor seating and a rooftop dining area. [Fig. 154] Thompson extended a ramp around three sides of the existing concrete block structure to provide principal access to the roof deck. She wrapped the ramp in a skin of spaced longleaf pine timbers, a particularly durable wood that was reclaimed from a nearby structure that the Parks Department had slated for demolition. The Warming Hut facilitates communal use of the park by providing amenities for visitors. For Van Valkenburgh, as for Thompson, the social functions of the park are primary; it anchors the area's residential neighborhoods and serves as a focal point in the daily lives of their inhabitants.

A third adaptive reuse park pavilion is Thompson's **Visitor Center for the Stevens-Coolidge House and Gardens** in

North Andover (2019–21), carried out as part of a phased expansion strategy for the historic property developed by Mikyoung Kim for the nonprofit conservation organization Trustees of Reservations. Here, Thompson transformed a former maintenance shed into a new visitors' entrance. [See Fig. 132] Large windows in the shed's open face overlook a terrace and adjoining meadow. She fitted the heavy-timber structure with a gift shop, a classroom, a snack bar, and restrooms. As with Thompson's other visitor centers, the pavilion facilitates public use of the ninety-one-acre site, the gardens and residence of which exemplify the region's historic horticulture and design traditions.

◆◆◆

Whether operating as a threshold to a site, as a destination, or serving in an educational or a recreational capacity, MTA's park pavilions and visitor centers contribute to the diverse experiences afforded by their landscapes. This reliance on architectural means to draw attention to the benefits of exposure to the natural environs enables Thompson to serve broader communal and environmental aims.

Figure 154 Pier 6 Warming Hut, Brooklyn Bridge Park (with MVVA)

Farms

A series of farm commissions prompted Thompson to draw upon her interest in vernacular forms—both for their expressive potential and for their commonsense means of energy conservation—in ways that would have significant repercussions for her architecture. Closely aligned with her park pavilions, visitor centers, and recreational structures, these projects enabled Thompson to expand upon her interest in integrating architecture and landscape to engage such issues as sustainable farming methods and public outreach, and to address environmental concerns.

Situated on a working farm in Washington State that overlooks the Olympic Mountains across the Strait of Juan de Fuca, the **Straitsview Barn** (Thompson and Rose, 1996–97) houses a farm office, wood and machine shops, a veterinary station, and a variety of large-scale equipment and machinery storage. [Fig. 155] Thompson derived several prominent features of her architecture from aspects of this commission, which she carried out in partnership with Charles Rose. The large, rolling barn doors of slatted wood were dimensioned to admit farm machinery and positioned to open directly onto the work yard [Fig. 156]. These oversized doors inspired Thomp-

Figures 155 & 156
Straitsview Barn, San Juan Islands, WA: exterior; sliding doors open to work yard

son to use similarly scaled sliding glass doors in her private residential commissions to optimize natural ventilation and enable the interiors to operate as seasonal screened porches.

The Straitsview Barn was her first use of heavy timber construction, commonly used on barns, nineteenth-century mill buildings, and related outbuildings throughout New England. The manner in which heavy timber framing renders the structural logic of the building visible and comprehensible to the occupants prompted her to employ this technique in various public projects. [See Figs. 13, 97, 110] The Straitsview Barn also exemplifies Thompson's propensity to take the site's climatic factors into account. Its L-shaped configuration deflects the prevailing northeastern winds that arise off the Pacific Ocean and shelters the adjacent work yard, which is bounded by a slatted wood fence that echoes the treatment of the barn doors in the adjoining facade.

The cedar shingle siding of the Straitsview Barn, like its exposed structural frame (made from reclaimed Douglas fir) and its slatted barn doors, derives from vernacular precedents. The rustic character of the shingled facades is amplified by the dappled sunlight that penetrates the veil of trees that were planted to shield the courtyard from direct solar exposure. Upon completion of the barn, the owners established conservation easements for the Straitsview Farm as part of the San Juan Preservation Trust in an effort to maintain the distinctive qualities of their two-hundred-eighty-acre property and its use as a working farm.

Figures 157 & 158
Drumlin Farm, Lincoln: renovated poultry barn; Farm Life Center interior

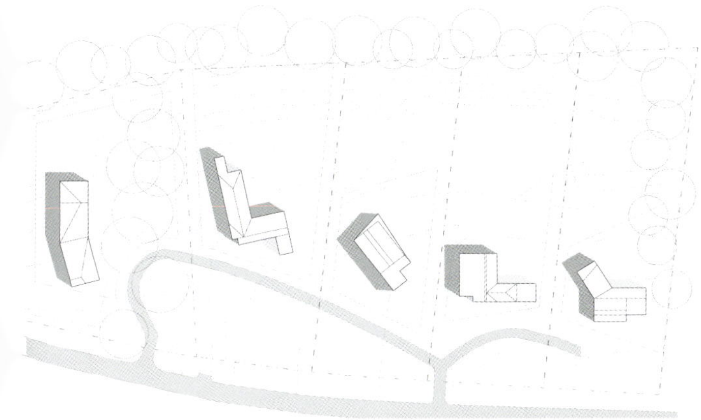

Figures 159 & 160
The Farm School, Athol: farmers' housing site plan; self-build farmer's house and barn

Vernacular precedents similarly inspired aspects of Thompson's other farm commissions in which broader educational, social, and environmental objectives prevailed. Beginning in 2005, MTA carried out a series of projects at Mass Audubon's working farm and wildlife sanctuary, **Drumlin Farm** in Lincoln, Massachusetts. Developed incrementally, without the benefit of a master plan, these began with the construction of a series of relatively modest structures—a poultry barn, a site entrance and farm stand, toilets inserted in an existing barn, and a pigsty—while fund-raising was underway for the **Farm-Life Center**, realized in 2008–11. [Figs. 157 & 158] The center's classroom and demonstration kitchen, which adjoins the vegetable garden, enabled Mass Audubon to expand its offerings of classes and programs promoting the benefits of sustainable agricultural methods and ecological consciousness. In keeping with the organization's environmental ethic, the high-performance building envelope includes super-insulated, triple-glazed windows, twelve-inch-thick walls, and ultra-tight construction. [See Fig. 129] Daylighting satisfies most lighting requirements thanks to a combination of ample south-facing windows, skylights, and a line of clerestory windows atop a light shelf that directs the incoming light upward to the ceiling, the curved form of which facilitates its even distribution. [See Fig. 121] Other energy-saving components include site-sourced and milled lumber used for siding, a state-of-the-art mechanical system with energy recovery, and a dedicated solar array added to both the goat shed and an existing sheep shelter.

Commissions from two private philanthropic organizations followed: the **Farm School** in rural Athol, Massachusetts, which offers instruction in agricultural practices for local children and students from Boston area schools, including overnight retreats and summer camps; and the **Slough Farm Foundation** on Martha's Vineyard, which promotes sustainable agricultural methods and animal husbandry, while providing support for local food equity organizations and creative endeavors.

For the **Farm School**, Thompson developed a master plan for a small segment of the four-hundred-acre site where the non-profit establishment provided land for five affiliated farmers and their families to build their own houses (2013–14). The proposal includes a site plan of the subdivided plots, indicating setbacks and view corridors. [Fig. 159] This layout and associated design protocols prioritize southern orientation for each residence in combination with further measures to optimize energy efficiency according to the principles devised by the Passivhaus Institut. Conversations with the farmers enabled Thompson to develop provisional layouts for five two-story houses, and MTA developed working drawings so that one of the farmers could realize a simpler self-build design. [Fig. 160]

Unlike earlier MTA projects for components of farm complexes, the commission from the philanthropic **Slough Farm Foundation** in Edgartown (2015–18) involved the design of complete farm facilities. To facilitate the permitting process, the components were built atop the footprints of the extant farm structures on the property, which had fallen into disrepair and required demolition. The foundation's communal aspirations prompted the program for the principal farm building, which includes a courtyard gathering space for classes, farmers' markets, and related public events and the Great Room (a dining hall with demonstration kitchen), along with accommodations for visiting artists, housing for the resident farmer and his family, and stalls for smaller animals. [See pp. 22–26]

The design incorporates variations on aspects of the Straitsview Barn: exposed heavy timber construction, with joints secured by large wooden pegs, and sliding barn doors in slatted wood that adjoin the Great Room's large, wood-framed sliding glass doors. Both projects share a similar concern for linking interior and exterior volumes. Aspects of Mass Audubon's Farm Life Center are recalled in the direct relationships among the demonstration kitchen, greenhouse, and vegetable garden, together with a reliance on reclaimed building materials. Other structures include a cow barn, an equipment barn, and an existing stave silo that was restored to serve as a beacon for the complex. [Fig. 161; see Fig. 17]

◆◆◆

Sited to take advantage of sun and wind orientations, and designed to emphasize interrelationships among different building components, these farm projects challenged Thompson to imagine the extent to which vernacular precedents might have bearing on the aesthetic, structural, and functional properties of her designs, especially in the Straitsview Barn, the outbuildings at Drumlin Farm, and the Slough Farm Foundation. In other cases, the reliance is more subtle, inspired by commonsense vernacular principles rather than adherence to any historic stylistic parameters.

Figure 161 Slough Farm Foundation, Edgartown, cow barn

Schools and Educational Venues

Designs for educational facilities comprise a significant aspect of Maryann Thompson's practice. Whether master planning, creating new buildings, or retrofitting existing structures, she begins each project by meeting with administrators, students, parents, trustees, and interested members of the public. The insights gleaned from the conversations that occur in these meetings often go beyond the written responses to her questionnaires, helping to clarify the attributes of a particular institution and the ways in which its various interested parties might envision potential future directions. Because Thompson considers the opinions of the students in these programs to be as significant as those of the commissioning clients, their insights are particularly valuable to her endeavors.

Because she understands the capacity for architecture to play an active role in the educational process, Thompson explores various ways in which the physical environment might aid in nurturing a student's inherent curiosity and foster encounters with the teaching staff as well with fellow classmates. [See pp. 44–65] Whenever possible, she seeks to accommodate multiple uses in each space. For example, she views the ubiquitous corridors that link classrooms as opportunities to accommodate individual or small group gatherings by varying their width and equipping them with seating and access to natural light. She also provides seating and play space outside her schools and daycare centers or just inside the entries, where parents might meet with other neighborhood parents and children or confer with staff members. [Fig. 162; see Figs. 116 & 117] A primary value of such gestures is their potential for

Figure 162 Jonathan Milikowsky Science and Technology Center, The Foote School, New Haven, seating at building entrance

Figure 163 Jonathan Milikowsky Science and Technology Center, science classroom

animating both the daily life of the institution and its civic value.

When a school's pedagogical stance extends to fostering respect for the environment and energy conservation, there are significant repercussions for the site and building layouts. The 2009 commission to design a new **Science and Technology Center** for **The Foote School** in New Haven (2009–12), for example, led Thompson to create a sustainable facility that restructures the organization of the entire middle school complex by optimizing relationships between her new facility and the existing campus buildings. **[See Fig. 36]** The architectural ramifications of this concern for environmental impacts include the widespread use of commonplace means of energy conservation, as well as more recent technological advances. An abundance of operable windows facilitates a reliance on natural daylighting and cross ventilation. These attributes are amplified by clerestory windows that also promote consciousness of the daily path of the sun and of temporal weather conditions throughout the building. **[Fig. 163]** The psychological effects of these forms are valued as much as their energy-saving properties.

Several of Thompson's commissions for educational facilities involve master planning, a process in which it is important to anticipate an institution's potential growth while accommodating its immediate needs. The reorganization of existing buildings often plays a significant role in these projects. For example, **Schools for Children**, a nonprofit organization in the Boston area dedicated to serving children with learning and behavioral difficulties, commissioned MTA to relocate and expand facilities for three of their programs (2016–19). When **Dearborn Academy** took over a former Catholic school building in Newton, Thompson subdivided the existing classroom layout to better serve the special needs students in that program, for whom small group interactions with a variety of support staff is a priority. For the **Lesley Ellis School**, MTA opened up the classrooms and the hallways of the former Dearborn Academy building in Arlington and fitted the corridors with seating to provide more flexible gathering spaces for groups of different sizes. **[Fig. 164]**

At the **Seaport Academy** in Chelsea, the limited amount of daylight emitted through the vertical openings in the five-foot-thick walls of the former Armory building inspired Thompson to use uplighting to draw attention to the existing stone vaults. [Fig. 165] In concert with her modest changes to the layout of small rooms that were formerly used as offices, this provided a comforting environment for the program's special needs students, as the confined spaces help to ease their sense of anxiety.

With her master plan for the **International School of Boston** (2011–12), Thompson identified fifty projects for the school's campuses in Cambridge and Arlington that could be completed incrementally during summer vacations. By 2018, construction on six of these projects had been completed. These included a library inserted in the turret of the main building on the school's Cambridge campus to take advantage of the heavy timber trusses that had been concealed during previous renovations, and the renovation of an adjoining convent that the school had purchased to accommodate additional classrooms. [Fig. 166] The success of these proposals led the International School to commission Thompson to design a new high school for their program, for which a property search is currently underway.

The larger, more open sites of certain educational commissions enabled Thompson to amplify relationships between architec-

Figure 164 Lesley Ellis School, Arlington, corridor renovation

Figure 165 Seaport Academy, Chelsea, classroom renovation

Figure 166 International School of Boston, upper school library

Figure 167 Visual and Performing Arts Center, Forman School, Litchfield, new academic green

ture and landscape. At the **Forman School** in Litchfield, Connecticut, she configured her **Visual and Performing Arts Center** (2015–17) to create a new academic green on the institution's south campus. **[Fig. 167; see Fig. 86]** The master plan for **The Ethel Walker School** in Simsbury, Connecticut (2021) entailed a more radical set of modifications. **[Fig. 168]** By shifting vehicular access to the campus periphery, rearranging the interiors of existing buildings, and adding several new structures, Thompson proposed to give definition to a sequence of external spaces that would augment the interrelationship of interior and exterior and prioritize pedestrian movement throughout the site.

Figure 168 The Ethel Walker School, Simsbury, master plan

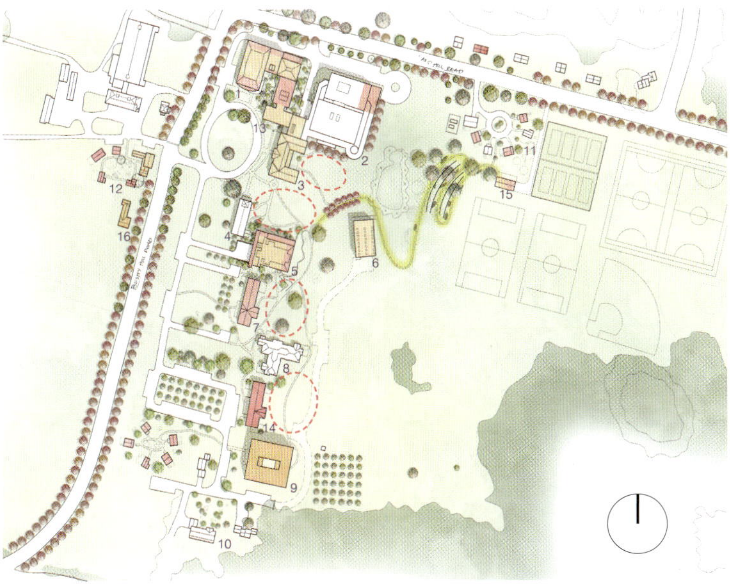

Several MTA projects have significant educational components, belying any strict programmatic classification of Thompson's creative output. These include the **Farm Life Center at Drumlin Farm**—a working farm and wildlife sanctuary for Mass Audubon—and a private foundation that is dedicated to advancing the cause of agricultural production, the **Slough Farm Foundation** in Edgartown.

◆◆◆

By devising specific architectural means to animate the learning environment, Thompson seeks to avoid the standard, repetitive forms found in conventional school designs. Whenever possible, she combines architectural specificity with programmatic flexibility. The variety in her educational projects derives from the educational philosophy of each institution as well as its specific programmatic requirements, the attributes of the site, the potential to amplify the role of external spaces in the educational environment, and the ways in which natural forces are brought to bear on her designs.

Restaurants

Thompson's restaurant commissions comprise interventions in existing buildings in which intimate spaces for dining are situated amid carefully orchestrated spatial sequences. Her designs vary according to each chef's intended ambiance, which ranges from formal and romantic at the Rialto Restaurant and Bar in Cambridge to the more casual domestic atmosphere of Pammy's, also in Cambridge. These restaurant commissions differ significantly from the dining amenities that comprise components of other MTA projects, such as the Great Room at the Slough Farm Foundation on Martha's Vineyard or the combination religious sanctuary and social hall at the Temple Ahavat Achim in Gloucester, where the communal character of each building program entailed the need for a flexible space for entertaining. **[See Figs. 19, 33 & 34]**

The award-winning chef Jody Adams commissioned three restaurants from MTA that differ substantially in character. The first, **Rialto Restaurant and Bar** (2006–07, no longer extant), had a quiet, romantic atmosphere befitting its location in the Charles Hotel in Cambridge. Thompson was allotted only six weeks—between the popular dates of New Year's Eve and Valentine's Day—to carry out the renovation of an earlier restaurant on the site. The entry sequence proceeded between the bar and a lounge to the dining room, where sheer floor-to-ceiling curtains were suspended from ceiling tracks to afford a sense of intimacy to the space without disrupting sightlines. **[Figs. 169 & 170]** To accommodate private events, two separate sections of the dining room could be closed off from the main space, in one case by folding glass doors, where a measure of privacy was assured by sheer curtains, and in the other by tall shutters that echoed those in the restaurant windows, where they were combined with curtains.

As with all of her restaurants, Thompson provided a variety of seating options. At Rialto, these consisted of dining nooks bounded on two or three sides by banquettes, upholstered chairs paired with square tables, and semicircular banquettes repurposed from the earlier restaurant, which she combined with circular tables and upholstered chairs. The varied heights of the banquettes amplified the relative sense of seclusion for each group of diners, which Thompson underscored by focusing recessed ceiling lights on the individual tables. The bar stools, chairs, and banquettes were covered in muted shades of green, brown, orange, and yellow velvet—a color palette that

Figure 169 & 170
Rialto Restaurant and Bar, Cambridge: entrance and bar; dining room

Figures 171 & 172
Rialto Restaurant and Bar: antipasto bar; lighting effects on curtains in bar seating area

was inspired by the variegated bark of the sycamore trees that line Memorial Drive. The abundance of soft surfaces served to muffle sound, contributing to the restaurant's intimate atmosphere.

Thompson used subtle lighting effects to distinguish among the restaurant's distinct zones and impart an aura of theatricality to the preparation of food and drinks. Cylindrical pendant lights suspended over the drinks bar were supplemented by uplighting below its onyx slab, which was edged in stainless steel so that the light seemed to emanate from both sides of its surface. [Fig. 169] This impression of the onyx as the source of the light made the bar appear to float above its canted base. To accentuate the performative aspect of food preparation, Thompson included a second bar to one side of the dining room where antipasti were prepared in full view of the diners. [Fig. 171] This bar top, formed with a deep slot below its uppermost surface, was fabricated from Carrera marble to reflect the bartender's hands as he prepared the appetizers. In a related example of indirect lighting, the recessed ceiling fixtures illuminated the curtains, which in turn lit the space. [Fig. 172] The layout of these unobtrusive ceiling fixtures was echoed in the strings of lights that hovered over the adjoining covered terrace, which were arranged to impart a suggestion of star light—an effect Thompson would reprise in her further commissions from Adams.

For her next restaurant, **Trade** (2010–11), Adams sought a more vibrant atmosphere, consistent with its downtown Boston location. Trade occupies the ground floor of a Renaissance Revival Building designed by Peabody and Stearns and realized in 1897 on the site of the former Russia Wharf. To capitalize upon the space's extant tectonic qualities, Thompson had the narrow brick ceiling vaults sealed and whitewashed, the concrete floor polished and stained dark amber, and the riveted steel columns painted white—with the exception of one column that marks the hostess station, which was painted saffron yellow. From the entrance, the open fire of a pizza oven is seen rising above the bar, imparting a domestic ambiance to the space. [Fig. 173] Thompson gave the bar an angled form so that it seems to dominate much of the room. Cloudlike segments

Figures 173 & 174
Trade, Boston: view from entrance to bar and pizza oven; restaurant seating with curved banquettes

of suspended ceiling that hover overhead give the volume a sense of intimacy. [Fig. 174] Serving practical as well as aesthetic ends, these soffit fragments conceal both a tangled web of pipes that emanate from the apartments above and a significant portion of the restaurant's mechanical equipment. Their abstract, immaterial appearance provides a start contrast to the ductwork, sprinkler system, and electrical conduits that are suspended from the exposed sections of brick vaulting. A related contrast pertains to the seating. The mobile tables and chairs in the vicinity of the bar are juxtaposed to a set of curved banquettes in the dining area. These are covered in saffron and green leather and backed by heavy wood spatial dividers to provide eddies of stability and calm within the general flow of the movement sequence.

At Trade, mirrors are used to achieve social as well as spatial ends. A line of fragmented mirrors above the bar affords patrons segmented glimpses of other customers, imparting an implicit sense of social connection among apparent strangers while distorting reflections of the restaurant's star-like field of small, circular pendant light fixtures. This line of mirrors extends over a wall of oak wine cabinets that separates the restaurant from the service zone, expanding the upper zone of the restaurant visually, and echoing the material contrast between the suspended soffits and the exposed ceiling. This thickened oak wall extends from the private dining room at one end of the restaurant to the restrooms at the other

Figure 175 Trade, bar seating with saffron yellow pendant lighting fixture

end. Concealed within its tongue and grove paneling are doors to the service areas and restrooms, effecting a material continuity that affords a sense of intimacy to the space. In keeping with Adams' interest in serving locally sourced food, much of the wood used in the design was repurposed and locally available. Further splashes of vibrant saffron yellow—a cypher for Adams—are found in the vertical stripes in the facade windows and the interiors of the large bowl-like metal ceiling fixtures that bathe the groups of diners seated at a round communal table and in an alcove off the bar in glowing fields of light. [Fig. 175]

The spacious site of Adams' third restaurant, Porto (2016), at the perimeter of the mixed-use Prudential Center in Boston's popular Back Bay neighborhood, enabled Thompson to draw upon certain ideas from her two earlier designs to create a markedly different atmosphere. After demolishing the dropped ceiling in the former office space, Thompson opted to expose segments of its concrete waffle slab, which are stained white to selectively expand the space upwards. A dominant feature at Porto is the presence of two bars—one serving drinks and the other for food preparation—which effectively subdivides the space into zones, each of which accommodate diverse forms of seating for single patrons as well as groups of various sizes. [Figs. 176 & 177] The drinks bar is supplemented by a rolling cocktail cart, used throughout the restaurant for tableside cocktail offerings, as well as by another bar on the adjoining dining terrace. As at Rialto, the performative aspect of the bifurcated kitchen, with limited openings between its bar and the bustling food preparation zone beyond, serves to foster a more direct relationship between patron and cooking staff, while the material palette of whitewashed brick, raw concrete, and natural woods is more closely aligned with that at Trade.

To evoke a seaside ambiance at Porto, which offers variations on Mediterranean fare, Thompson used an indirect lighting system devised by the German industrial designer Ingo Maurer. Although the light seems to emanate from the delicate crystals suspended in flowing arcs of netting that are hung from the exposed ceiling, the actual light sources are concealed in the corners of these voids. [Fig. 178] This reliance on the ephemeral quality of indirect lighting prioritizes the spatial effects of lighting over the object quality of the light source.

Thompson credits restaurant co-owners Pam Diem and Chris Willis with the

Figures 176 & 177 Porto: drinks bar; food preparation bar

Figure 178 Porto, dining area with Ingo Maurer lighting fixture

distinctive character of their restaurant, **Pammy's**, in Cambridge (2016–17). Sited in a single-story brick structure between Harvared and Central Squares, Pammy's combines the relaxed, home-like character of a "New American trattoria" with chef Chris Willis's sophisticated take on Italian cuisine.[1] Diners are greeted by a colorful twenty-foot-long peacock mural by the children's book illustrator Rebecca Walsh that extends from the building entrance into a corner of the lounge. **[Fig. 179]**

Thompson's design includes large industrial windows inserted in the facade. She contrasted the existing interior walls of exposed brick with segments of lustrous Venetian plaster and introduced a double-faced fireplace in white ceramic tile between the lounge and the dining area. **[Fig. 180]** These elements, together with the long brown leather banquettes that line the dining room, set the stage for the Thonet café chairs and marble-topped tables that Thompson used to complement the owners' eclectic collection of salvaged objects that were incorporated in the project. These include a large, gilt-framed mirror, pendant lighting fixtures, and a statue of Demeter, the Greek goddess of the harvest who keeps watch over the bar. Diem and Willis also conceived of the long central table, a communal gesture that was fabricated using wood pieced together from old wooden drafting tables. **[Fig. 181]** A marble strip down the center holds an assortment of antique jugs that are filled with flowers

1 See pammyscambridge.com

Figure 179 Pammy's, Cambridge, mural at entrance

to afford the diners a measure of privacy. Unlike Thompson's proclivity to capitalize on the structural features of the ceilings at Trade and Porto by contrasting them with her architectural interventions, at Pammy's she left the wood frame roof structure fully exposed. The celling and the HVAC ducts that Thompson discretely inserted between the purlins are all painted forest green, thus muting the ceiling's industrial qualities by giving it the uniform appearance of a backdrop for the light that emanates from the pendant light fixtures. These patterned glass globes refract the light emitted by the bulbs to create the subtle effect of glowing orbs, which is supplemented by the beams of light emitted by the spreading arms of the pendant light fixture over the communal table.

◆◆◆

Despite the varied character and material palettes of these restaurants, they each offer a range of seating options that afford diverse degrees of intimacy for the diners, while manifesting Thompson's creative use of lighting to amplify the specific atmospheric qualities.

Figures 180 & 181
Pammy's, view from bar to dining room; communal table

Houses

Maryann Thompson conceives of the private residence as a nurturing environment in support of the particular lifestyles and aesthetic proclivities of her clients. Toward that end she begins each house commission with a questionnaire to identify their needs and interests on a range of topics, including material preferences, the relationship between interior and exterior, preferred vistas, and attitudes toward sustainability, as well as the daily routines of the family. Because Thompson values the manner in which her designs draw upon the changing conditions of natural light, she inquires as to where her clients tend to spend time over the course of the day. The variety in her residential designs derives from the diverse contexts in which they are situated (suburban or rural), whether they involve the transformation of existing structures or new construction, and whether they are primary residences or vacation homes, as well as from the prolonged conversations that follow upon the responses to her questionnaires. In this highly collaborative and iterative design process, the homeowners' suggestions often play a significant role in the outcome. Owing to the degree of intensive engagement with her clients, Thompson considers residential design to be a particularly satisfying type of commission.

The relationship of interior to exterior and to the broader context of a site is a primary focus of Thompson's residential work. She consistently seeks architectural means to heighten awareness of the physical and temporal qualities of the natural environs. Toward that end, her designs begin from a careful consideration of the locale—its natural features, topography, and orientation to the daily path of the sun and to the prevailing winds, as well as opportunities for vistas. In a related vein, MTA's residences generally feature commonsense passive methods of energy conservation, many of which derive from vernacular design traditions. These include ample operable windows to enhance daylighting and provide cross ventilation (often supplemented by ceiling fans), deep thresholds to mediate the transition from interior to exterior through roof overhangs positioned to provide protection from the summer sun and admit the warmth of the lower-lying sun in winter, and operable clerestory windows to draw out excess heat through the stack effect and amplify consciousness of the daily path of the sun throughout the interior. Certain examples also take advantage of recycled and energy-efficient materials or recent technological advances such as photovoltaic systems to

Figure 182 Bluff House, Edgartown, aerial view

generate electricity and geothermal HVAC systems. Thompson brings the importance of environmental sustainability to bear on these designs at scales that range from site planning to the materials and forms of architectural systems.

Thompson's residential designs are characterized by unfolding spatial sequences in both their vehicular approaches and their internal circulation routes that continually reorient the occupants and their visitors to interrelationships among the architecture, the immediate landscape, the distant prospects, and the sky. Situated on a windblown locale overlooking the Atlantic Ocean, for example, the **Bluff House** in Edgartown (2004–07) operates as an expanded threshold between the saltwater ponds to the north and the Atlantic Ocean to the south, a condition that is accentuated by its numerous windows oriented to the views. [Fig. 182] The grounded quality of the house's stone plinth contrasts the light trapezoidal forms of its roof, drawing attention to the relationship of ground to sky. This emphasis on the vertical dimension is reiterated in clerestory windows that span between the angled roof planes, which admit varying conditions of natural light into the depth of the building. [Fig. 183] A similar material contrast characterizes the **Watcha Pond House** in West Tisbury (2014–17), the layout of which draws upon the ocean views from the upper level as well as those to the pond from both floors. [Fig. 184]

Several of MTA's vacation houses consist of detached structures, whether main house and guest house, residence and studio, or group living spaces and bedrooms. In addition to insuring privacy for the daily lives

Figure 183 Bluff House, view to entrance

Figure 184 Watcha Pond House, West Tisbury, view from east

Figures 185 & 186 Egret Meadow House, West Tisbury: view from guest house to principal residence and bedroom pavilion; living/dining/kitchen

Figure 187 Pamet Harbor House and Studio, Truro, view from south

of the residents and their guests, this tactic optimizes access to views while enabling the built volumes to remain subsidiary to the natural features of the site, and facilitates natural ventilation throughout the interior. For example, the **Egret Meadow House** in West Tisbury (2011–14) has distinct family and sleeping quarters linked by a covered breezeway. A separate guest house lies to the southeast. [Fig. 185] Large, aluminum-framed sliding glass doors enable the rooms of the three single-story structures to open broadly onto terraces that afford views to a branch of the Tiasquam River to the southwest. [Fig. 186] The resulting natural ventilation is amplified by the stack effect, which derives from clerestory windows that line the northeastern facade. In common with the Egret Meadow House, **The Oaks** in West Tisbury (2007–13) features a separate master bedroom, guest house, and garage. Further examples with a detached guesthouse include **West Hill** (2017–24) and the **Watcha Pond House**, while those that combine a residence and studio include the **Think House** in Silver Lake, Vermont (2005–06), and the **Pamet Harbor House** in Truro (2009–10). [Fig. 187]

Thompson's design for a commercially available prefabricated house, co-sponsored by *Dwell* magazine and Empyrean International, constitutes a variation on this idea. Now marketed by the Acorn Deck House Company, the **Hinge House** (2008) is sold as a kit of parts that are precut in the factory and delivered to the site for assembly. It consists of two primary components that can be variously configured to accommodate shared family functions and bedrooms or the principal residence and a garage or guest house, for example. The wings are rotated about a "hinge" point to form an outdoor

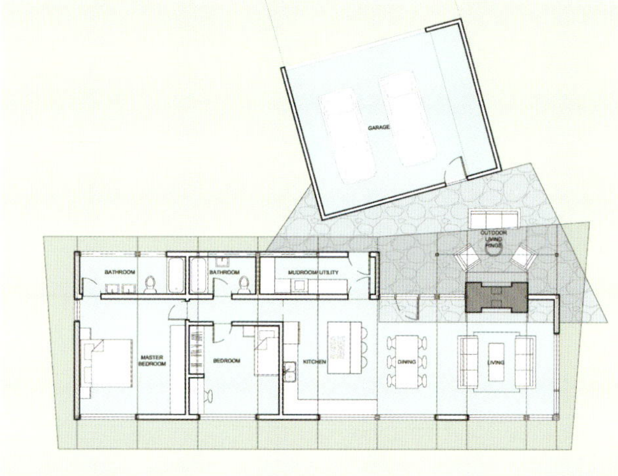

Figures 188 & 189
Hinge House: plan for two bedroom option with garage; perspective rendering of "hinge" outdoor living space

living space with a fireplace, which Thompson envisioned as a fulcrum of activity at the heart of the residence [Figs. 188 & 189]. For a variation realized outside Washington, D.C., MTA worked with the client to develop the design and fit it to the site. Because the flexible layout of the Hinge House can be adapted to the individual needs of the owner and to varying topographic conditions, it is ideally suited to take advantage of passive design principles, including optimal orientation to the sun and prevailing winds.

Several of Thompson's vacation houses feature outdoor decks at different levels. These diverse spaces for entertaining, dining, or more secluded activities—such as reading, sunbathing, quiet contemplation, or enjoying a sunlit outdoor shower—take advantage of outlooks to the immediate and distant landscapes. Cascading decks off both the bedrooms and living spaces of the **Pamet Harbor House** and **Fallen Leaves** in Aquinnah (2001–04) exemplify Thompson's proclivity for drawing upon their seaside locales to integrate the experiences afforded by her architecture with those of the natural environs. [Fig. 190] At Fallen Leaves, a low mound rises to a mid-level entry, from which an internal stair rises another half level around the end of a massive fireplace to a combination living/dining room and kitchen on the uppermost level, where the distant water views are brought into focus.

To similarly take advantage of the views available from an elevated position at **60 Slough** (2015–17), a summer residence off of Slough Cove in Edgartown, Thompson placed the bedrooms at the entry level and the principal living space on the uppermost floor. Two small sitting areas—one inside the front door and the other off the bedrooms—provide spaces for informal family gatherings along the route from the entrance to the open living/dining room and kitchen on the floor above. [Figs. 191 & 192] Owing to the need to match the footprint and volume of an earlier house on the site, she employed a large triangular window under the pitched roof to frame the view to Slough Cove, making the water a relatively immediate presence in the space.

Many of Thompson's vacation houses are characterized by a propensity to enable the collective family spaces to open fully to the exterior and operate as screened porches. [Fig. 193] Two smaller examples demonstrate

Figure 190 Fallen Leaves, Aquinnah, view from the northwest

Figures 191 & 192 60 Slough, Edgartown: upper level living/dining/kitchen; entry level gathering spaces

Figure 193 & 194
Marsh House, Chappaquiddick, and West Hill Guest House, Orange, showing open living/dining/kitchen serving as seasonal screened porch

this phenomenon of the residence as a seasonal screened porch: the **Small House** in Great Barrington (2006–10) and the **West Hill Guest House** in Orange (2015–16). [Fig. 194] In each, open layouts can be compartmentalized to ensure privacy for the sleeping quarters.

Thompson frequently collaborates with Michael Van Valkenburgh on her houses in Martha's Vineyard, where both have summer homes. His elaboration of the landscape, like that of the architecture, varies according to the conditions of the site and the proclivities of the owners. At **Cove House**, another private residence on Slough Cove (2015–17), Van Valkenburgh combined a respect for the ecological importance of the area's sandplain grasslands—a rare and imperiled ecosystem that the Nature Conservancy is striving to maintain—with intricate garden areas in the immediate vicinity of the house. [Fig. 195] His landscape scheme for **Fallen Leaves** is simpler and more abstract. The house is sited in a grassy clearing amid densely wooded environs. To conceal the wintertime views of a neighbor's residence from the ground floor bedrooms, Van Valkenburgh created a curving landform, which he planted with bamboo. To demarcate the juncture between the lawn and the surrounding woodland and frame the distant views of Vineyard Sound from the upper levels of the house, he relied on the simple, repetitive use of tall grasses.

In contrast, Van Valkenburgh's interventions at **The Oaks** are so subtle that they might easily escape the purview of residents and visitors alike. [See Figs. 82–84] Inspired by the site's dense oak woodland, he worked with Thompson and her clients to devise a long, winding entry drive that reveals the presence of the house only momentarily as the road rises to a parking area that adjoins a garage and guest house. Consistent with Thompson's inclination to conceive of her architecture as subsidiary to its site, she wrapped the wings of the residence around a small, grassy knoll at the top of the hill, so that the experience of the dappled light that pierces the tree canopy and falls on the fern- and moss-covered forest floor remains a dominant feature of both the vehicular approach and the movement sequence lead-

ing up to, through and beyond the house. This sense of immersion in the forest along a route that concludes in a deck beside a giant oak tree contrasts with the experience at **Fallen Leaves**, where ascent to the open living/dining level culminates in expansive views to the wooded environs to Vineyard Sound and the Elizabeth Islands.

◆◆◆

In each of Thompson's houses, the forms operate in service to a particular quality of life. Despite certain similarities in materials and details, her houses differ considerably in the ambiances they evoke. These differences result not only from the extensive participation of her clients in the design process, but also from the way in which Thompson draws inspiration from the particular qualities of each site. They are further amplified when her architectural response is interwoven with that of the landscape architect with whom she is collaborating.

Figure 195 MVVA, Cove House, Edgartown, "river" of perennials traversed by footbridge

Terry Real

Fallen Leaves: Living in Art

166

Not a day goes by that either my wife, Belinda, or I don't express gratitude for the gift of living inside our "Maryann house." And we secretly believe that, of all her vacation houses, including numerous sprawling eight-figure examples, our little 2,300-square-foot beach house is the unnamed jewel, her love child—and ours. [Fig. 196]

Here's the backstory. We were a young family with just enough saved for a beautiful four acres on a bluff in Aquinnah, Martha's Vineyard. We knew Maryann from our kids' school; we'd grown to like each other. She had just launched her own practice and sought to develop her portfolio. We needed a house. Maryann bent over backwards to make the house affordable, and we were involved every step along the way. The skylight that I sit under as I write this was created at my insistence—though making it a flaring triangle was sheer Maryann. [Fig. 197] Belinda doubled the size of our outside decks, then Maryann doubled the height of our screened porch, making it soar. [Fig. 198] I should say from the start that the whole house soars in a way. It feels nautical, or perhaps like a space cruiser.

From the upper reaches of the house the vista extends over an extensive stand of trees, leading in turn to the Vineyard Sound, the Elizabeth Islands, and, in the distance, to the lights of New Bedford, the old whaling town. With a crank between the upper-level living/dining room and the master bedroom, Maryann literally wrapped our house around this view, making it accessible from every room.

Figure 196 Fallen Leaves, Aquinnah, view from the northwest

Figures 197 & 198 Fallen Leaves: living/dining room threshold to deck; screened porch

Access to nature is primary. There seems little distinction between inside and out. In our living room, huge floor-to-ceiling glass doors slide open so that the space of the room is echoed again in the adjoining deck, just a step away. Then the trees, then the Sound. And the sky. And the weather. Oh my, New England weather. We can lounge on our living room couch beside a roaring fire with drinks in our hands and watch a storm blow in from the mainland. The wind screams and lightening sears the sky around us as thunder rattles the trees. It feels like we're inside a Beethoven symphony, safe and secure in our wood and glass ship.

Our bedroom is essentially a light-filled cube that combines expansive views to the Sound and the sky with the warmth of a fireplace. [Fig. 199] It recalls one's childhood delight at camping under the stars—only warm and dry. And our third-floor deck—our ship's bridge, my summer "office"—enables us to feel like we're at the beach without the sand, within easy reach of ice or a bathroom. Under our cantilevered umbrella we can park ourselves on that deck for the better part of a day, then bring up food, libations, and friends in the evenings.

With so much wide-open space, both inside and out, the house absorbs a cocktail party-sized crowd with no problem. Our guests admire my barbecue and smoking palladium off the lawn, where their children play badminton or croquet. A Buddhist calm and peacefulness resides here. Belinda's interiors are a genius we've labeled "Zen Cozy." A comfortable,

Figures 199 & 200 Fallen Leaves: master bedroom; kitchen

lived-in minimalism. Under Maryann's encouraging eye, Belinda's talent for design unexpectedly blossomed. Every surface of this house, ranging from the stone for the living room fireplace to the sea-glass green of the kitchen countertops, was selected with loving care by the two of them—a perfect collaboration. [Fig. 200]

Every place the eye rests is beautiful, from the weightless corner window in the kitchen that gives views onto the garden to another high up in the master bathroom that looks up to the face of the moon. The materials that were weighed, discussed, and chosen by our little team exude a sensuous quality, from the great smell of the bamboo floors to the heat that emanates from the stucco fireplace. Light streams in everywhere, layers of glass, rows of glass, light upon light.

Throughout the house we feel both immersed in nature and cosseted at the same time; it is like the most elegant, secure, crystalline diving bell imaginable. And curious creatures do appear—a multitude of rabbits, birds, and deer come to visit. Our house is a place of equal parts beauty, tranquility, protection, and gorgeously executed exposure. After sixteen years living inside our soaring glass ship, it still feels like an adventure.

Doug Reed

Westport Meadow House: An Evocation of Place

Touch this earth lightly.
Glenn Murcutt (2000)

When one looks at Nature through the glass walls of the Farnsworth House, it takes on a deeper significance than when one stands outside. More of Nature is thus expressed—it becomes part of a greater whole.
Mies van der Rohe (1958)

Every day, the great horizontal reach of our home in Westport, Massachusetts grabs me, holds me, and fills me with a sense of wonder and solace, no matter what season of the year. It is a familiar feeling for me, one that emerged from impressionable childhood days spent in Louisiana's delta landscape, where the pervasive flatness of the land—the result of repeated flooding and soil deposited over the millennia by the Mississippi River—extends to the horizon. [Fig. 201] The ground, when measured by the geometric order of its crops and the fluid forms of its flooded rice fields, has an abstracted quality of an almost incomprehensible scale. The enduring riparian and agrarian character of the Westport site stems from a similar layering of natural features and those that derive from acts of human intervention, and it too is indelible. [Fig. 202] Both places have profoundly shaped me in my work as a landscape architect. For reasons I can't fully explain, this continui-

Figure 201 Louisiana Rice Fields

ty of landscape character across the early and later years of my life brings me deep comfort and reassurance.

Some twenty years ago, my husband Will Makris and I acquired these forty-three acres along Westport River's East Branch, six miles north of Buzzards Bay. Before we embarked on the design of a house, we spent several years getting to know the place, seeking to discover why the landscape looked like it did. On our frequent visits to the site, we experienced the dynamic weather patterns that are characteristic of south coastal Massachusetts: the luminous atmosphere that arises when land, clouds, and sky take on the sunlight refracting off of the bay; the shadows that rake across the gentle undulations of ground; the nearly ever-present wind; and the rain and the abundant fog that can be penetrating. There were no dwellings on the site. There was a nineteen-acre field, but it was surrounded on all sides by rampant invasive vegetation that smothered a quarter-mile stretch of river bank and occluded views of the distant landscape in every direction. Each weekend we rented equipment to edit the unwanted vegetation. With each incremental act of removal, remarkable views opened up to adjacent fields, stone walls, woods, and the river corridor. These experiences deepened our love for the site, because here we came to feel connected to a larger natural system; we sensed that we belonged to something much bigger than ourselves.

It was Maryann's pursuit of contemporary architecture as a vehicle for capturing and engaging ecological phenomena that resonated with us and motivated us to commission her to design our home. The warmth and openness of Maryann's character seized us, and she related to Will and me with complete equality. Her point of view and way of working, which I had experienced in previous collaborative endeavors, seemed pertinent to our desire to make a sanctuary for our lives here. She also understood how important it was for us to share the place with family and friends in the hope that it would inspire and transport our guests as much

Figure 202 Westport Meadow House, view to historic stone boundary wall

as ourselves. Over the years the property has encouraged our visitors to write, photograph, paint, celebrate, and join us in our love of growing crops and cooking.

The predominant identity of the Westport project lies in its sweeping expanse of meadow, river, and sky. Paradoxically, the horizontality of the site that I found so compelling and evocative, and which Maryann identified as the power and promise of the project, was in fact created by the destructive operations of sand and gravel mining that gouged the landscape over a hundred years ago. The meadow's broad and idyllic condition that one sees today obscures the results of these operations that fundamentally altered the site's ecology. The excavation of some thirty feet of rolling land left a depleted and irregular terrain of tailings and massive erratics (glacially deposited rocks), many of which can be seen throughout the lowland woods and along the river's edges. It was only through subsequent decades of effort by a nearby farmer to reclaim nineteen acres of the depleted land and build up the soil to support crops that we have the gift of today's meadow to nurture and to experience as the focus of our house.

The serene pastoral beauty of this designed landscape belies dualities in the site's character—between stability and disturbance, permanence and transience, order and chaos. The sleepy, meandering course of the river, the occasional ancient trees cloaked in lichens, and the vestiges of stone walls and hedgerows that stem from nineteenth-century agricultural patterns elicit a feeling of stability and endurance. We protect and tend to these features that predate our tenure here. In contrast, the meadow is fleeting, dynamic, unpredictable, animated. Each year its plant composition differs strikingly, depending on the amount of seasonal moisture, the harshness of the winter, the seed that blows in from nearby fields, and when and how I mow. [Figs. 203–205] Over the years, we haven't introduced a single plant; instead, we manage the vegetation to maximize species diversity, suppress invasive plants, and attract birds and insects. These dualities pose compelling challenges as we attempt to manage the inevitable changes in this landscape. Sometimes we work to adhere to our initial design intentions, maintaining and managing components of the original scheme; at other times we accept the changes brought on by nature's processes, adjust our intentions, and respond with new design solutions. In these ways landscape design exemplifies a kind of creative work in perpetual progress, guided by governing ideas yet requiring shifts in their expression to meet the inev-

Figures 203-205
Westport Meadow House, mowed paths through landscape during different seasons

itable and unpredictable changes of a living medium—a process that couldn't be more different than that of producing a work of architecture.

Within this context, Maryann conceived of a 2,200-square-foot house and a 900-square-foot guest house and garage, which is rooted in precedents of early twentieth-century houses by Richard Neutra, Marcel Breuer, Rudolph Schindler, and others, and in the abstract spatial qualities that she explored for their relevance to our way of life and to the land. The project brought together Maryann, interior designer Thad Hayes, and my landscape architecture firm, Reed Hilderbrand. In her creative process, Maryann sought critical information about our program, values, and aspirations, which she elicited not only through written responses to her questions but more importantly through her profound empathy for our interests and concerns. We enjoyed Maryann's remarkable balance of intuition and rigor in the pursuit of her work, the nimble flexibility of her thinking, and her genuine openness to ideas—qualities that generated a steadfast trust among ourselves and the various members of the team. The collaboration resulted in a seamless integration of a house and its landscape as it hovers over a gently sloping meadow and captures views of river, land, and sky.

There is a modesty to the house in this expanse of open land, far beyond the fact that it is a small house. Maryann sought an architecture deferential to the site. After considering several locations in the meadow, we agreed to place the house two hundred feet from the river's edge, some six feet below the meadow's highest elevation, which would enable it to sit low in the gently undulating landform. Oriented roughly parallel to the course of the river, this location directly engages the East Branch and its tree-lined banks, and it captures a wide, two-mile-long oblique view to the south down the corridor of the river as it drifts toward the bay.

The layout and massing of the house attest to Maryann's conviction in the power of the site's horizontality. [See Fig. 99] A linear composition of attenuated rooms is organized to either side of a three-foot-wide wood-clad zone that stretches the length of the building and holds the utilities, storage, closets, and some appliances. This internal aggregation of programs that require opaque enclosure enabled the rooms to either side of it to be walled in glass, opening in multiple directions to views of the landscape and its ever-changing character.

Given the house's open plan, Maryann elected to modulate the height of the rooms to create alternating spatial experiences of compression and release, hide and reveal. We took cues from this spatial articulation for our interventions in the landscape, designing a path network to take us through similarly contrasting spatial experiences of the property. It leads from open sunny areas to the deep shade of hedgerows and woods, along the riverbank with its expansive views, and back to vegetated areas that are more intimate and focused. This compelling and varied sequence satisfies our love of walking, as the mowed paths that extend from the house's numerous exit points draw us through the property on our encounters with nature's daily changes.

The expanses of glass along the perimeter of the house bring not only transparency but also reflection and refraction, which serve to dematerialize the structure and to generate a spatial ambiguity between inside and outside. [See Figs. 101 & 102] Maryann understands the use of glass during the early phases of modernism, which revolutionized architecture's engagement of the landscape. We seized the opportunity to draw upon this aspect of her design by strategically siting trees to extend the interior volumes and capture outdoor space within their realm. [Fig. 206] Just as their trunks frame outward views to the landscape, so their canopies serve to extend the horizontal plane of the ceilings. With our house I now more fully understand Philip Johnson's notion that trees form "the basic building material" of his Glass House in New Canaan, Connecticut.[1]

Maryann further qualified the distinction between interior and exterior by choosing materials for certain indoor

[1] Philip Johnson cited in Hillary Lewis and John Connor, *Philip Johnson: The Architect in His Own Words* (New York: Rizzoli International Publications, Inc., 1994), 34.

Figure 206 Westport Meadow House, view along the south-western facade

surfaces that are typically associated with exterior conditions—galvanized steel columns, concrete, cedar siding, and marine-grade plywood. For the interiors, Thad expanded on this idea by drawing upon the site's rural character in selecting furniture made from American Beech, floors of white oak, nubby fabrics, and an earthy color palette derived from the mottled bark of the sycamores that we planted to shade the house. [See Figs. 93–95] In such a place—where change is embraced through structures designed to serve as part of, and as a foil for, natural phenomena—serendipity prevails. After a few months of living in the house, I told Maryann that she had created a vessel for capturing light and atmosphere.

Many of our visitors have described the experience of the house as one of living on a porch. The nearly flat roof planes extend to protect areas of wooden decking for outdoor living and circulating and to shelter the house from the western and southern exposures; these accentuate its horizontality and enable the house to appear to settle into the meadow. We live much of the time in these outdoor areas, designed to extend from the interior at such a height above the meadow to afford views to the horizon. [Fig. 207; see Fig. 101]

Our Westport home brings us great joy and satisfaction as a unified work of architecture and landscape design where the historical, cultural, and ecological systems of the site coalesce to become an integral part of our daily lives. We see our aspirations and values embodied in this place. We fully embrace our roles as stewards in caring for the health and beauty of the land and maintaining the integrity of Maryann's structures. We learn immeasurably from these considered acts of domesticating the land, which have become ritualized over the years. They nurture us, ground us, and make us feel that we belong here. [Fig. 208]

Figure 207 Westport Meadow House, deck sitting area.

Figure 208 Westport Meadow House, view from the riverfront

Maryann Thompson in Conversation

Landscape and the natural world are an important part of your design process. Where does that interest come from?

Maryann Thompson I grew up on a farm in Ohio. As a child, I found deep solace in the surrounding landscape. The patterns, textures, and light were immersive. They transformed the scenery, which left a formative impression. That quintessential Midwest setting—being outdoors constantly amid nature—instilled a sense of psychological safety.

Being immersed in nature brought me a profound sense of comfort. I'm always trying to recreate that feeling of sanctuary from my youth. The "forest bathing" movement completely resonates with me: surrounding yourself in densely vegetated spaces provides an embracing, nurturing sensation akin to being hugged by the woods' edge.

Certain trees held special significance. My magical-thinking sister got us believing the maple syrup taps were ways to communicate with tree spirits when we were little. Viewing the landscape through that lens of wonder, where nature teemed with life forces protecting us, made for an enchantingly whimsical childhood. Like on Christmas Eve when she'd insist the animals could talk, so we'd await their voices expectantly.

Those formative experiences outdoors as a child, engaging nature's mysteries and magic, laid the foundations for how I understand the world.

With such a deep connection to nature, why didn't you become a landscape architect? At what point did architecture become an influence and a path?

MT My dad wanted to be an architect, but his father pressured him to work in the family business. He had an affinity towards and love of buildings. We would go to Columbus, Indiana, a wonderful place full of modern architecture whenever a new building was constructed. It was a two-hour drive from our home and on one of those trips I discovered the work of landscape architect Dan Kiley—who worked in collaboration with a lot of the architects there, particularly Eero Saarinen. I saw how the landscape influenced the building, and vice-versa.

My father also took me to the Hyatt in San Francisco—which I later discovered was by John Portman. We walked in, and that giant atrium with the plants cascading down from floating platforms was amazing. We were so excited about it—a landscape integrated into architecture! So, because of his influence and curiosity, I was immersed in architectural explorations and discussions throughout my childhood.

Do you have a philosophy that anchors your work?

MT Those early experiences really made an impression, and I try to heighten experiences of landscape in the work, or through the work. It's way of practicing architecture that heightens the direct human experience of the site and the landscape: the sun, the rain, breezes, and the way the light enters the building. Though each of my projects look different, issues and themes of landscapes and nature are consistent.

I also try to express the woven quality of architecture through tectonics and details, so that the effects of the sun create dappled, rippling light. That expression also reflects an honesty about how architecture is made: it's a woven art form.

I think of architecture as part of a natural system. This idea is evident in the way we work with natural ventilation. Operable windows bring the breeze and create a stack effect. When heated air rises it pulls the colder, fresher air in from the ground. The canopies—the deep overhangs that function as shading devices—are never purely stylistic. They are operative and performative, organized towards the sun, and provide shade on the south-facing and west-facing windows—but they are dynamic like a tree canopy.

In the education projects there is a phenomenological methodology, but there's also a pedagogical model embedded in the designs. What is your approach to school building projects.
I love that you recognize this as a systematic scientific approach, even though it may seem only aesthetic at first glance. It's about understanding how natural forces like wind and sun create forms, and then working backwards from there.

Many educators want to help children feel more connected to the outdoors. They feel that kids are too disconnected from nature—stuck in school buildings without much recess or outdoor time. I get requests from schools wanting to bring more of the outside in. For the Montessori school they wanted one big, open room. We designed a 10,000-square-foot space with splayed roofs to let the sun penetrate deep into the floorplan.
While the end result does have an aesthetic appeal, it's fundamentally grounded in pragmatic scientific principles about how natural systems like light, air flow, and thermal massing function. Articulating the built environment to harness these forces creates comfortable, sustainable interior spaces connected to the outdoors.

I'd like to be able to directly influence how most children learn. I think I can do that through public school commissions which, in Massachusetts, serve up to two thousand kids at a time. That's a much larger scale than the schools that I've created so far, but that's the direction I'd like to move things. It's the right next step. There's a real commitment to sustainability with a public school system, so it aligns with what I'd like to do.

We've been talking about conditions of light and air, but these elements rely on the nature of materials for the effects to be felt. How do you approach materiality?

MT This is really important to me. My sensibilities are informed by the work of architect Kiel Moe, whose ideas have resonated deeply. When I read his writings, I felt "Yes, that's exactly the way I feel." His concepts and writings on thermally active surfaces explain why wood feels so pleasant. Our bodies are on the same resonant frequency as wood, so it doesn't draw heat away like glass or metal. It just feels neutral, like touching a body.

Wood has a warmth beyond just temperature—the colors and textures contribute, too. I like contrasting wood with other materials to heighten the experience. Interiors with only wood can sometimes feel overwhelming. The interplay of wood with glass, stone, and plaster is interesting—the same ambient temperature, but distinct thermal interactions. These insights helped put in practice what I intrinsically felt about the coziness of wood interiors. Understanding the science deepens the appreciation.

How has your relationship with longtime collaborator Michael Van Valkenburgh evolved over the years?

MT Michael was my professor at the GSD, and I worked in his office. He helped me launch my practice by introducing me to my first client. It made sense to start an ongoing collaboration with Michael—we're very similar in approach; he also cares about the process of being immersed in nature.

One of the great joys of my life is the experiences I've had working with Michael. The collaborative process with him is both joyful and thoughtful. As he creates, he also teaches, so it is often a learning experience to work with him. He is a force of nature, a deep, creative font—a person who sees deeply into sites, drawing out their potential for beauty and inspiration through a heightening of their regional spirit. And working with him is fluid, because we sketch back and forth, and his sketches are really loose and beautiful.

I try to create work that's equally immersive and haptic. Like him, my landscapes and buildings hopefully create a sense of wonder and awe. We curate these senses through unfolding sequences of movement and view. Every time you move, you're in dialogue with the building, with the landscape.

CONTRIBUTORS

Shantel Blakely is assistant professor at the Rice University School of Architecture, where she teaches architectural history and design studios. Her research is concerned with architecture and architectural practice in the U.S. and Europe from 1945 to the present. She is the author of a book on the Italian architect and industrial designer Marco Zanuso, which is forthcoming at the time of this publication, as well as numerous journal articles. Her research in progress on the St. Louis African-American architect Charles E. Fleming is supported by the Getty Research Institute and the Graham Foundation for Advanced Studies in the Fine Arts. Between her studies at Princeton University (M Arch) and Columbia University (PhD), she worked at Thompson and Rose Architects (1999–2000) and Maryann Thompson Architects (2000–01).

Caroline Constant is Professor Emerita of the University of Michigan, where she taught from 2001 to 2013. A fellow of the American Academy in Rome, she is author of numerous books and articles on the interrelationship of architecture and landscape architecture, including *The Modern Architectural Landscape* (2012), *The Woodland Cemetery: Toward a Spiritual Landscape* (1994), and *The Palladio Guide* (1985). She is author of *Eileen Gray* (2000) and co-editor of *Eileen Gray: An Architecture for All Senses* (1996), for which she was named an Honorary Member of the Royal Institute of the Architects of Ireland. Maryann Thompson was her student and teaching assistant at the Graduate School of Design, Harvard University, where Constant was Associate Professor of Architecture (1983–92).

Martha Foss, AIA, is a licensed architect and principal of MTA, where she has been directing projects since 2005. A graduate of the University of Virginia (BS Arch) and Yale University (M Arch), she is a LEED accredited professional and Certified Passive House Designer of the Passivhaus Institut. She has taught architecture studios at Yale University, Syracuse University, Wentworth Institute of Technology, and Northeastern University, among other institutions.

Terry Real is an internationally recognized family therapist, teacher, and author. In 1997, he founded the Relational Life Institute, offering online workshops for couples, individuals, and parents around the country along with a professional training program for clinicians wanting to learn his Relational Life Therapy methodology. His books include *I Don't Want to Talk About It: Overcoming the Secret Legacy of Male Depression* (1997); *How Can I Get Through to You? Closing the Intimacy Gap Between Men and Women* (2002); *The New Rules of Marriage: What You Need to Know to Make Love Work* (2008); and *US: Getting Past You and Me to Build a More Loving Relationship* (2022).

Douglas Reed, FASLA, is a founding partner of the award-winning landscape architecture firm Reed Hilderbrand and a frequent collaborator with MTA. The practice is known for designing landscapes at a variety of scales that weave a site's history and its ecologies with programmatic imperatives to forge inventive and relevant contemporary spaces. Reed is a recipient of the ASLA Design Medal, which recognizes a career of exceptional design work. In 2011 he was recognized as a Resident of the American Academy in Rome. Reed is a founding board member of The Cultural Landscape Foundation and co-author, with Gary Hilderbrand, of the firm's monograph *Visible Invisible: landscape works of Reed Hilderbrand* (2012).

Maryann Thompson, FAIA, is founding principal of Maryann Thompson Architects, a practice that specializes in architecture that is sustainable and regionally driven. With professional degrees in architecture and landscape architecture from the Harvard University Graduate School of Design, Thompson is committed to heightening the experiential qualities of each project and its broader context, whether urban or natural, through a holistic, consensus-building approach to design. The firm includes professionals trained in architecture, landscape architecture, green architecture, planning, interior design, and the visual arts. Prior to founding MTA in 2000, Thompson was a founding partner of Thompson and Rose Architects (1991–2000). At the Graduate School of Design, she was visiting critic in landscape architecture (1995–96), design critic in architecture (2001–07), adjunct professor of architecture (2007–13), and Professor of the Practice of Architecture (20013–17). She has also served as a visiting faculty member at the Massachusetts Institute of Technology, the Rhode Island School of Design, the University of Virginia, the University of Michigan, and Rice University. For her distinguished contributions to architecture and to the profession, the Boston Society of Architects presented Thompson with its Award of Honor in 2024.

PROJECT CREDITS

CIVIC AND CULTURAL INSTITUTIONS

Leeper Studio Complex, Atlantic Center for the Arts, New Smyrna Beach FL (Thompson and Rose, 1989–97)
T&R principals Charles Rose, Maryann Thompson
Landscape Architect Hanson Taylor Bellomo Herbert, Glen Herbert
Structural Engineer Oemulgee Associates, Wayne King
Contractor Epoch Properties
Awards Florida AIA Honor Award, Test of Time
AIA 20th Year Award Finalist
AIA National Design Honor Award
AIA New England Design Honor Award
ID Design Distinction Award
BSA Honor Award for Design Excellence
BSA Unbuilt Architecture Award

Whitehead Institute, Cambridge MA (renovation, 2003–04)
MTA Project Manager Missy Grisnik
Structural Engineer Shooshanian Engineering, Inc.
Contractor F. L. Caulfield and Sons, Inc.

Zero Arrow Theater, Cambridge MA (renovation, 2004–05)
MTA Project Managers David Martin, Tom Murdough
Contractor Martini Construction
Awards Boston's Best Theatre, Improper Bostonian, 2008

Eli and Edythe L. Broad Institute, Cambridge MA (2004–06)
MTA Role Design Architect
Architect of Record Elkus Manfredi
MTA Project Manager David Martin
MTA Project Support Tom Murdough, Ania Matteson
Contractor Kirkland Construction Co. Inc.

Temple Ahavat Achim, Gloucester MA (2009–12)
MTA Project Manager Martha Foss
MTA Project Support Zac Cardwell, Rachel Stevens
Structural Engineer RSE Associates
Contractor Kaplin Construction

H3 Biomedicine Lab (Esai), Cambridge MA (renovation, 2010–11)
MTA Project Manager Zac Cardwell
Laboratory specialists Olson Lewis Dioli & Doktor Architects
Contractor The Richmond Group

First Parish Church, Lincoln MA (addition, 2013–18)
MTA Project Manager Zac Cardwell
MTA Project Support Tim Carey, Tom Murdough, Rebecca Rahmlow
Structural Engineer Roome & Guarracino LLC
Interior Design Kenneth E. Hurd & Associates, Inc.
Contractor Charles Construction Company Inc.

Lincoln Community Center, Lincoln MA (2017–18, 2022)
MTA Project Manager Martha Foss
MTA Project Support Sydney Cinalli

Follen Community Church, Lexington MA (addition and renovation, 2017–20)
MTA Project Manager Doug Jack
MTA Project Support Katie Chu, Kaitlin Kurs, Brittany Milas, Stephanie Morrison, Jeff Vogel
Structural Engineer Roome and Guarracino LLC
Contractor ZVI Construction

Congregation B'nai Israel, Northampton MA (addition and renovation, 2018, 2021–)
MTA Project Manager Christine Hefferen
MTA Project Support Ben Meyers, Adam Murfield

Vineyard Haven Public Library, Vineyard Haven MA (addition and renovation, 2019, 2024–)
MTA Project Manager Gentley Bondeson
MTA Project Support Jeffrey Dike, Kenneth Mendez, Yasmine Perez
Structural Engineer Sourati Engineering, Inc.

Science for America, Cambridge MA (renovation, 2023–)
MTA Project Manager Gentley Bonderson

Sunbridge Amenity Center and Housing, Osceola County FL (2023–)
MTA Project Manager Jeffrey Dike

PARK PAVILIONS AND VISITOR CENTERS

NARA Park Bathhouse and Amphitheater, North Action MA (Thompson and Rose, 1998–2000)
T&R Principals Charles Rose, Maryann Thompson
Contractor E. A. Colangeli Construction
Awards Boston Society of Architects Design Honor Award
AIA New England, Award for Design Excellence

Leventritt Garden Pavilion, Arnold Arboretum, Boston MA (Thompson and Rose/MTA, 1997–2002)
T&R Principal Maryann Thompson
MTA Project Manager David Suttle
Landscape Architect Reed Hilderbrand
Structural Engineer RSE Associates
Contractor Lee Kennedy Co., Inc.
Awards AIA New England Design Award
Boston Society of Architects Design Citation
Boston Society of Architects Unbuilt Design Honor Award
ASLA Award of Excellence

Visitor Center, Polly Hill Arboretum, West Tisbury MA (Thompson and Rose/MTA, 1999–2001)
T&R Principal Maryann Thompson
T&R Project Manager Franco Ghilbardi
Landscape Architect Michael Van Valkenburgh Associates, Inc.
Structural Engineer Ocmulgee Associates
Contractor Coast Construction
Awards AIA New England Honor Award for Design Excellence
BSLA Design Honor Award

Corktown Common Pavilion, Toronto, Ontario CA (2006–11)
MTA Project Manager Hope Strode
MTA Project Support Bill Pevear
Landscape Architect Michael Van Valkenburgh Associates, Inc.
Structural Engineer RSE Associates
Contractor Eastern Construction
Awards 2017 Urban Land Institute Global Award for Excellence (MVVA)
ASLA Professional Awards, Honor Award for Design (MVVA)

Pier 6 Warming Hut, Brooklyn Bridge Park, Brooklyn NY (adaptive reuse renovation, 2006–11)
MTA Project Manager Evan Mathison
MTA Project Support Bill Pevear
Landscape Architect Michael Van Valkenburgh Associates, Inc.
Structural Engineer RSE Associates
Contractor Skanska USA Building Inc.
Awards Architizer A+ Awards, Special Mention

Pier 2 Recreation Pavilion, Brooklyn Bridge Park, Brooklyn NY (adaptive reuse renovation, 2006–14)
MTA Project Manager Evan Mathison
MTA Project Support Tom Murdough, Bill Pevear
Collaborating Architect Lisa Easton
Landscape Architect Michael Van Valkenburgh Associates, Inc.
Structural Engineer RFR Engineering Consultants
Contractor Skanska USA Building Inc.
Awards AIA New York Design Award
Architizer A+ Awards in Community Design
AIA New England Design Citation
World Architecture News Adaptive Reuse Award

Walden Pond Visitor Center, Concord MA (2011–16)
MTA Project Manager Zac Cardwell
MTA Project Support Jeffrey Dike, Caroline James, Brittany Milas
Master Planner Crosby Schlessinger Smallridge
Landscape Architect Michael Van Valkenburgh Associates, Inc.
Structural Engineer RSE Associates
Contractor Stutman Contracting, Inc.
Certifications LEED Gold, Net Zero Energy
Awards Boston Society of Architects Accessible Design Honor Award
APR International Award for Sustainable Architecture (Cultural)
Wood Design Awards, Wood in Government Buildings

Walden Pond Bath House, Concord MA (2018–)
MTA Project Manager Zac Cardwell
MTA Project Support Jeffrey Dike, Reihaneh Ramezany
Landscape Architect Crosby Schlessinger Smallridge
Structural Engineer RSE Associates

Visitor Center, Stevens-Coolidge House and Gardens, North Andover MA **(adaptive reuse, 2019–21)**
MTA Project Manager Martha Foss
MTA Project Support Doug Jack, Kelsey Margulies
Landscape Architect Mikyoung Kim Design
Structural Engineer Dan Bonardi Consulting Engineers
Contractor Joset Corp

Long Hill and Sedgwick Gardens, Beverly MA (masterplan, 2019)
MTA Project Manager Martha Foss
MTA Project Support Katie Chu
Landscape Architect Mikyoung Kim Design

Charlesbank Landing Pavilion, Charles River Esplanade, Boston MA **(2017–18, 2023–)**
MTA Project Manager Zac Cardwell
MTA Project Support Katie Chu, Benjamin Bromberg Gaber, Yasmine Perez
Landscape Architect Michael Van Valkenburgh Associates, Inc.
Structural Engineer RSE Associates

Brighton Public Pool Complex, Brighton MA (masterplan, 2021–23)
MTA Project Manager Zac Cardwell
MTA Project Support Solomon Rosenthal
Structural Engineer RSE Associates
Landscape Architect Verdant

Morses Pond Bathhouse, Wellesley MA (2022–)
MTA Project Manager Zac Cardwell
MTA Project Support Katie Chu
Landscape Architect Weston and Sampson

Kapor Foundation, Edgartown, Martha's Vineyard MA (2022–)
MTA Project Manager Jeff Vogel
MTA Project Support Kenneth Mendez, Yasmine Perez

Visitor Center, Botanical Garden of the Piedmont, Charlottesville VA (2023–)
MTA Project Manager Martha Foss
MTA Project Support Reihaneh Ramezany, Amy Vaughan
Landscape Architect Mikyoung Kim Design
Structural Engineer Springpoint Structural

FARMS

Straitsview Barn, San Juan Island WA (Thompson and Rose, 1996–97)
T&R Principals Charles Rose, Maryann Thompson
Landscape Architect Michael Van Valkenburgh Associates, Inc.
Structural Engineer B & B Engineered Timber
Contractor S.B. Inc.
Awards AIA National Honor Award
Boston Society of Architects Honor Award for Design Excellence
American Wood Council Design Honor Award

Drumlin Farm Wildlife Sanctuary for Mass Audubon, Lincoln MA (2005–11)

Poultry Barn (renovation, 2005–07)
MTA Project Manager John Mucciarone
Contractor Cyril Hughes

Entry Plaza and Farm Stand (2007–08)
MTA Project Manager Hope Strode
Structural Engineer RSE Associates
Contractor Cyril Hughes

Restrooms at the Red Barn (addition, 2007–08)
MTA Project Manager Hope Strode
Structural Engineer RSE Associates
Contractor Cyril Hughes

Farm Life Center (2008–11)
MTA Project Manager Hope Strode
MTA Project Support Brittany Milas
Structural Engineer RSE Associates
Sustainability Consultant Marc Rosenbaum, Energysmiths
Contractor Marulli and Son General Contractors
Certifications LEED Gold, Net Zero Energy

The Farm School, Athol MA (master plan for farmer's housing, 2013–14)
MTA Project Manager Katrina Stoll Szabo

Slough Farm, Edgartown, Martha's Vineyard MA (2015–22)

Master plan (2015–18)
MTA Project Managers Konstantine Papadimitrakopoulos, Doug Jack
MTA Project Support Katie Chu, Gregory Logan, Ricardo Solar
Landscape Architect Michael Van Valkenburgh Associates, Inc.

Foundation Building and Farmer's Residence (2016–18)
MTA Project Managers Konstantine Papadimitrakopoulos, Doug Jack
MTA Project Support Katie Chu, Gregory Logan, Ricardo Solar
Landscape Architect Michael Van Valkenburgh Associates, Inc.
Structural Engineer Sourati Engineering Group
Contractor Tate Builders Inc.

Cow Barn, Equipment Barn, and Greenhouse (2017–18)
MTA Project Managers Konstantine Papadimitrakopoulos, Doug Jack
MTA Project Support Katie Chu, Gregory Logan, Ricardo Solar
Structural Engineer Sourati Engineering Group
Contractor Tate Builders Inc.

Central Field Barn and Community Space (adaptive reuse renovation, 2020–22)
MTA Project Manager Douglas Jack
Structural Engineer Sourati Engineering Group
Contractor Wolftone Construction LLC

Farmers' Co-Housing (2023–)
MTA Project Manager Gentley Bonderson
MTA Project Support Katie Chu, Konstantinos Papadimitrakopoulos
Landscape Architect Michael Van Valkenburgh Associates, Inc.
Structural/Green Engineer Energylogik
Owner's Representative Cristina Schieren

SCHOOLS AND EDUCATIONAL VENUES

Chilmark Elementary School, Chilmark MA (Thompson and Rose, 1994–2001)
T&R Project Manager David Whitney
Contractor Standon Contracting Company

The Children's School, Stamford CT (2003–07)
MTA Project Manager Martha Foss
MTA Project Support David Martin, Ania Matteson, James Steel, Tamar Warburg
Collaborating Architect Ingrid Strong
Structural Engineer RSE Associates
LEED Consultant Green Roundtable
Contractor Viking Construction
Certifications LEED Certified
Awards American School and University William W. Caudill Citation for K-12 Facilities Design Awards
Design Share School Design Forum Merit Award.
Boston Society of Architects Educational Facilities Honor Award for Design Excellence
Boston Society of Architects Sustainable Design Honor Award for Design Excellence
American Institute of Architects New England Merit Award

The Atrium School, Watertown MA

Lower School (adaptive reuse renovation, 2005–06)
MTA Project Manager William Pevear
MTA Project Support Zac Cardwell, Evan Mathison, John Mucciarone
Landscape Architect Landworks Studio
Structural Engineer RSE Associates.
Sustainability Consultant Green Engineer
Contractor Bowdoin Construction Corporation
Awards Hanley Wood Evergreen Award
Boston Society of Architects Honor Award for Design Excellence
AIA New Hampshire Honor Award for Design Excellence
IDID Excellence in Sustainable Design Award
Design Share School Design Forum Merit Award
American School & University Special Citation
Eco-Structure Magazine Evergreen Award for Adaptive Reuse

Middle School (adaptive reuse renovation, 2010–12)
MTA Project Manager Daina Swagerty
Structural Engineer Buro Happold
Contractor Bowdoin Construction

New Canaan Community Nursery School, New Canaan, CT (renovation and addition, 2008–10)
MTA Project Manager Marie Adams
Structural Engineer Hallama and Pellicione LLC
Contractor RSM Construction LLC
Awards The New Canaan Preservation Alliance Inc. Award

Jonathan Milikowsky Science and Technology Center, The Foote School, New Haven CT (2009–12)
MTA Project Manager Martha Foss
MTA Project Support Zac Cardwell, Michelle Laboy, Ryan Lemmo
Owner's Representative Leland Torrence Enterprises
Structural Engineer RSE Associates
Contractor Chapel Construction
Awards Boston Society of Architects Sustainable Design Award
Boston Society of Architects Educational Facilities Award

Early Learning Center for Novartis Pharmaceuticals Corporation, East Hanover NJ (2012–15)
MTA Project Manager Martha Foss
MTA Project Support Ben Franceschi, Michelle Laboy, Adam Murfield
Landscape Architect Michael Van Valkenburgh Associates, Inc.
Structural Engineer Buro Happold Consulting Engineers
Contractor Whiting-Turner Contracting Company
Awards Boston Society of Architects Education Facilities Citation

Shady Hill School, Cambridge MA (master plan, 2012–13)
MTA Project Manager Michelle Laboy
MTA Project Support Katie Chu, Martha Foss
Energy Use Analysis Buro Happold Consulting Engineers

Cambridge Center for Adult Education, Cambridge MA (renovation, 2012–14)
MTA Project Manager Stephanie Morrison
MTA Project Support Brittany Milas
Structural Engineer Roome and Guarracino
Awards Massachusetts Historic Commission Historic Preservation Award
Cambridge Historic Commission Award

International School of Boston, Cambridge MA (2011–)

Master plan (2011–12)
MTA Project Manager Michelle Laboy

Ninth Grade Lounge (renovation, 2011–12)
MTA Project Manager Michelle Laboy
MTA Project Support Ben Francheschi, Ryan Lemmo, Daina Swagerty
Structural Engineer Buro Happold Consulting Engineers
Contractor Highland Development, Inc.

Upper School Library (renovation, 2011–13)
MTA Project Manager Michelle Laboy
MTA Project Support Ben Francheschi, Ryan Lemmo, Daina Swagerty
Structural Engineer Buro Happold Consulting Engineers
Contractor Highland Development, Inc.

Middle School (renovation, 2012–13)
MTA Project Manager Michelle Laboy
Contractor Highland Development, Inc.

Lower School (renovation, 2013–14)
MTA Project Manager Michelle Laboy
Contractor Highland Development, Inc.

Faculty Lounge and Lobby (renovation, 2014–15)
MTA Project Manager Martha Foss
Contractor Storrow Company

Convent conversion to classrooms (renovation, 2015–18)
MTA Project Manager Benjamin Meyers
MTA Project Support Gregory Logan
Landscape Architect Hartney Greymont
Structural Engineer Roome & Guarracino
Contractor Storrow Builders, ZVI Construction

Lower School Library (renovation, 2021–23)
MTA Project Manager Kenneth Mendez
MTA Project Support Benjamin Meyers
Contractor Damon Smith

Princeton University Child Care Center, Princeton NJ (2013–18)
MTA Project Manager Michelle Laboy
MTA Project Support Katie Chu, Victoria McGovern
Landscape Architect Michael Van Valkenburgh Associates, Inc.
Structural Engineer RSE Associates
Energy Consultant Atelier Ten
Contractor Irwin and Leighton Commercial Builders
Certifications LEED Gold

Forman School Visual and Performing Arts Center, Litchfield CT (2015–17)
MTA Project Manager Stephanie Morrison
MTA Project Support Douglas Jack, Victoria McGovern
Owner's Representative Leland Torrence Enterprises
Structural Engineer Roome and Guarracino, LLC
Contractor A.P. Construction Company

Forman School Fab Lab, Litchfield CT (addition, 2016)
MTA Project Manager Douglas Jack
MTA Project Support Victoria McGovern
Structural Engineer Toce Structural Engineering, LLC
Contractor Woodmaster Building

Schools for Children (2016–19)

Lesley Ellis School, Arlington MA (renovation, 2016–19)
MTA Project Manager Benjamin Meyers
Structural Engineer DM Berg Consultants
Contractor ZVI Construction

Dearborn Academy, Newton MA (renovation, 2016–19)
MTA Project Manager Benjamin Meyers
Structural Engineer DM Berg Consultants
Contractor ZVI Construction

Seaport Academy, Chelsea MA (renovation, 2017)
MTA Project Manager Benjamin Meyers
Structural Engineer DM Berg Consultants
Contractor ZVI Construction

MGM Head Start and Family Center, Springfield MA (2017–18)
MTA Project Manager Zac Cardwell
Structural Engineer RSE Associates
MEP and FP Engineer Garcia-Galuska-DeSousa Consulting Engineers, Inc.
Contractor D.A. Sullivan and Sons, Inc.
Certifications LEED Platinum
Zero Energy Certification from the Living Future Institute
Awards Boston Society of Architects Sustainability Design Award

Ethel Walker School, Simsbury CT (2021–)

Master Plan (2021)
MTA Project Manager Gentley Bondeson
MTA Project Support Kelsey Margulies
Owner's Representative Leland Torrence Enterprises

Upper School Dormitory (2021–24)
MTA Project Manager Martha Foss
MTA Project Support Gentley Bondeson, Christina Hefferan, Kelsey Margulies, Reihaneh Ramezany
Owner's Representative Leland Torrence Enterprises
Structural Engineer RSE Associates
Contractor A.P. Construction Company

Advancement Offices (renovation, 2021–)
MTA Project Manager Christina Hefferan
MTA Project Support Gentley Bondeson, Kelsey Margulies, Reihaneh Ramezany
Owner's Representative Leland Torrence Enterprises
Contractor A.P. Construction Company

Dede Thompson Bartlett Center for Admission and Career Education, Vassar College, Poughkeepsie NY (2021–)
MTA Project Manager Benjamin Meyers
MTA Project Support Christina Hefferan, Gregory Logan, Matthew Moffitt, Yasmine Perez
Structural Engineer Murray Engineering

President's House, Olin College of Engineering, Needham MA (addition and renovation, 2021–24)
MTA Project Manager Jeffrey Dike
MTA Project Support Kenneth Mendez, Yasmine Perez, Solomon Rosenthal
Structural Engineer Dan Bonardi Consulting Engineers
Contractor ZVI Construction

RESTAURANTS

Rialto Restaurant and Bar, Cambridge MA (renovation, 2006–07)
MTA Project Manager Martha Foss
MTA Project Support James Steel, Jenny Tjia
Contractor Cafco Construction Management

Trade Restaurant, Boston MA (adaptive reuse renovation, 2010–11)
MTA Project Manager Michelle Laboy
MTA Project Support Ryan Lemmo, Jon Miller
Contractor Cafco Construction Management

Porto Restaurant, Boston MA (adaptive reuse renovation, 2016)
MTA Project Manager Adam Murfield
MTA Project Support Benjamin Meyers, Eleonora Peretti
Contractor Ashling Inc.

Pammy's Restaurant, Cambridge MA (adaptive reuse renovation, 2016–17)
MTA Project Manager Brittany Milas
Collaborating Architect Derek Bloom
Contractor Stack and Co.
Awards Boston Globe Restaurant of the Year
Best New Restaurant, Best of Boston 2018

HOUSES (SELECTED)

Fayerweather Street House, Cambridge MA (adaptive reuse renovation, Thompson and Rose/MTA, 1998–2002)
T&R Principal Maryann Thompson
T&R/MTA Project Support Shantel Blakely
Landscape Architect Michael Van Valkenburgh Associates, Inc.
Structural Engineer Ove Arup & Partners
Contractor Marvel Construction

Geothermal House, Belmont MA (2001–03)
MTA Project Manager Bill Pevear
MTA Project Support Tom Murdough, David Suttle, Ioana Urma
Structural Engineer Siegel Associates, Inc.
Contractor S+H Construction
Awards Boston Society of Architects Honor Award for Design Excellence
Boston Society of Architects Housing Awards Citation.

Fallen Leaves, Aquinnah, Martha's Vineyard MA (2001–04)
MTA Project Manager Bill Pevear
MTA Project Support Tom Murdough, Ioana Urma
Landscape Architect Michael Van Valkenburgh Associates, Inc.
Structural Engineer Siegel Associates, Inc.
Contractor Pizzano Construction

Westport Meadow House, Westport MA (2002–05)
MTA Project Manager Tom Murdough
MTA Project Support Derek Johnson
Landscape Architect Reed Hilderbrand
Structural Engineer Robson and So Engineering
Mechanical Engineer Marathon Engineers
Contractor Kendrick Snyder Builders
Awards Boston Society of Architects Honor Award for Design Excellence
AIA Honor Award for Design Excellence

Zero Impact House, North Easton MA (2004–06)
MTA Project Manager Bill Pevear
MTA Project Support Ania Matteson
Structural Engineer RSE Associates
Contractor CDS Construction Services
Certifications LEED Gold

Bluff House, Edgartown, Martha's Vineyard MA (2004–07)
MTA Project Manager Tom Murdough
MTA Project Support Zac Cardwell
Landscape Architect Michael Van Valkenburgh Associates, Inc.
Structural Engineer RSE Associates
Contractor Richard Karski, K.C.O. Builders

Grove House, Newton MA (renovation, 2004–07)
MTA Project Managers Evan Mathison, Jenny Tjia
MTA Project Support John Mucciarone
Landscape Architect Michael Van Valkenburgh Associates, Inc.
Structural Engineer RSE Associates
Contractor Denali Construction

Stonington Ridge House, Stonington CT (2004–08)
MTA Project Managers David Martin, Bill Pevear
MTA Project Support Richard Broene, Meredith Dontello, Martha Foss, Christine Napolitano, James Steel, Alexis Sparko
Landscape Architect Reed Hilderbrand
Structural Engineer RSE Associates
Contractor Denali Construction

Pamet Harbor House, Truro MA (renovation, 2004–10)
MTA Project Manager Michelle Laboy
MTA Project Support John Mucciarone
Structural Engineer RSE Associates
ContractorA. F. Hultin & Co., Inc.

Deer Meadow,Jacksonville VT (2005–06)
MTA Project Manager Martha Foss
Contractor Gary Bloom

One + One = One, Chestnut Hill MA (renovation, 2006–07)
MTA Project Manager Zac Cardwell
Contractor Marvel Construction

Hilltop Glade, Truro MA (2006–08)
MTA Project Manager Zac Cardwell
Structural Engineer Felco Engineering
Contractor Augustus Construction

The Small House, Great Barrington MA (2006–10)
MTA Project Manager Evan Mathison
Structural Engineer RSE Associates
Contractor The Small Building Company
Awards Boston Society of Architects Honor Award for Design Excellence

Traill Street House, Cambridge MA (renovation, 2007–09)
MTA Project Manager Michelle Laboy
Contractor Hughes Construction Inc
Awards Boston Society of Architects Award for Design Excellence

East Hampton Pool Pavilion, Wainscott NY (2007–09)
MTA Project Manager Martha Foss
MTA Project Support Christopher Karlson
Landscape Architect Reed Hilderbrand
Structural Engineer RSE Associates
Contractor Ben Krupinski Builders

The Oaks, Chilmark, Martha's Vineyard MA (2007–13)
MTA Project Manager Rachel Stevens
MTA Project Support Bill Pevear
Landscape Architect Michael Van Valkenburgh Associates, Inc.
Structural Engineer RSE Associates
Contractor Holmes Hole Builders

Hinge House, Acorn Deck House Company, Acton MA (prefabrication proposal, 2008)
Realized version, Accokeek MD (2009–13)
MTA Project Manager Evan Mathison

Marsh House, Chappaquiddick, Martha's Vineyard MA (2009–15)
MTA Project Manager Rachel Stevens
MTA Project Support Zander Auerbach
Structural Engineer Roome & Guarracino, LLC
Contractor Holmes Hole Builders

Valley Spring, Newton MA (renovation, 2011–13)
MTA Project Manager Zac Cardwell
Structural Engineer RSE Associates
Contractor Marvel Construction Corporation

Egret Meadow House, West Tisbury, Martha's Vineyard MA (2011–14)
MTA Project Manager Ryan Lemmo
Landscape Architect Reed Hilderbrand
Structural Engineer Buro Happold
Sustainability Consultant Marc Rosenbaum, Energysmiths
Contractor Holmes Hole Builders

Clark Hill, Belmont MA (2012–15)
MTA Project Manager Ben Franceshi
MTA Project Support Evan Mathison, Brittany Milas, Katrina Stoll-Szabo
Structural Engineer Roome and Guarracino
Contractor Groom Construction

Smoketree House, Somerville MA (renovation, 2013–14)
MTA Project Manager Ryan Lemmo
Structural Engineer Dan Bonardi Consulting Engineers
Mechanical Engineer TE2 Engineering
Contractor Marvel Construction

Eagles Flight, Dover NH (2014–16)
MTA Project Manager Stephanie Morrison
MTA Project Support Tim Carey
Structural Engineer Dan Bonardi Consulting Engineers
Contractor Don Walden, General Contractor

Watcha Pond House, West Tisbury, Martha's Vineyard MA (2014–17)
MTA Project Manager Martha Foss
MTA Project Support Ben Franchesci, Benjamin Meyers, Stephanie Morrison, Elenora Peretti
Structural Engineer Rist-Frost-Shumway Engineering, P.C.
Contractor Bannon Custom Builders

60 Slough, Edgartown, Martha's Vineyard MA (renovation, 2015–17)
MTA Project Manager Katie Chu
MTA Project Support Doug Jack
Landscape Architect Michael Van Valkenburgh Associates, Inc.
Structural Engineer Sourati Engineering Group
Contractor Tate Builders Inc.

Cove House, Edgartown, Martha's Vineyard MA (renovation, 2015–17)
MTA Project Manager Doug Jack
MTA Project Support Martha Foss, Kaitlin Kurs
Landscape Architect Michael Van Valkenburgh Associates, Inc.
Structural Engineer Sourati Engineering Group
Contractor Tate Builders Inc.

Enders-Klinkenborg House, Barn, and Studio, East Chatham NY (2015–18)
MTA Project Manager Adam Murfield
MTA Project Support Ben Meyers
Landscape Architect Michael Van Valkenburgh Associates, Inc.
Structural Engineer Frost-Shumway Engineering, P.C.
Contractor Ristiale Brothers Construction, Inc.

West Hill, Orange MA (2015–)

Guest House (2015–16)
MTA Project Manager Zac Cardwell
MTA Project Support Katrina Stoll-Szabo
Structural Engineer Rist-Frost-Shumway Engineering, P.C.
Mechanical Engineer Sun Engineering
Contractor Fred Heyes

Studio (2017–20)
MTA Project Manager Katie Chu
Structural Engineer Dan Bonardi
Contractor Damien McNally

Main House (2021–24)
MTA Project Manager Katie Chu
Structural Engineer RSE Associates
Contractor Charles Bado

Abel's Hill Treehouse, Chilmark, Martha's Vineyard MA (renovation, 2017–19)
MTA Project Manager Benjamin Meyers
Structural Engineer Sourati Engineering Inc.
Contractor Autumn Construction

Lincoln River House, Lincoln MA (2017–19)
MTA Project Manager Martha Foss
MTA Project Support Tim Carey
Structural Engineer RSE Associates
Contractor Bannon Custom Builders

Ocean Glen Cove, Edgartown, Martha's Vineyard MA (2018–20)
MTA Project Manager Gentley Bondeson
MTA Project Support Katie Chu, Martha Foss, Kelsey Margulies
Structural Engineer Sourati Group Engineering
Contractor Holmes Hole Builders

Ocean Meadow House, Newport RI (2019–23)
MTA Project Manager Jeff Vogel
Structural Engineer Dan Bonardi Consulting Engineers
Mechanical Engineer Consulting Engineering Services LLC
Contractor Bannon Custom Builders

Gurney Street Dell House, Cambridge MA (2019–23)
MTA Project Manager Martha Foss
MTA Project Support Katie Chu, Kelsey Margulies, Matt Moffit
Landscape Architect Matthew Cunningham Landscape Design LLC
Structural Engineer RSE Associates
Sustainability Consultant Marc Rosenbaum (Energysmiths)
Contractor Essex Restoration

Dune House, Aquinnah, Martha's Vineyard MA (renovation 2020–22)
MTA Project Manager Jeffrey Dike
MTA Project Support Zac Cardwell, Ben Meyers
Landscape Architect Michael Van Valkenburgh Associates, Inc.
Structural Engineer Martha's Vineyard Engineering & Design
Contractor Holmes Hole Builders

Secret Garden House, Newton MA (2020–24)
MTA Project Manager Konstantine Papadimitrakopoulos
MTA Project Support Matthew Moffitt, Yasmine Perez, Solomon Rosehthal
Structural Engineer RSE Associates
Contractor Bannon Custom Builders

Farmer's Residence, Straitsview Farm, San Juan Island WA (2021–)
MTA Project Manager Kelsey Margulies
Structural Engineer RSE Associates

Edgartown Bay House, Edgartown, Martha's Vineyard MA (2021–)
MTA Project Manager Katie Chu
MTA Project Support Sydney Cinalli

Raymond Street House, Cambridge MA (2021–24)
MTA Project Manager Zac Cardwell
Structural Engineer Fergal Brennock, P.E.
Landscape Architect Verdant Landscape Architecture

Stone House Earthship, Wendell State Forest, Wendell MA (2021–)
MTA Project Manager Katie Chu
Contractor Damien McNally

MTA STAFF

Marie Adams
Meghan Archer
Sean Arkin
Zander Auerbach
Sela Bailey
James Beasley
Autusa Behroozi
Assia Belguedj
Abraham Bendheim
Shantel Blakely
Charlotte Boghossian
Gentley Bondeson
Rick Broone
Deidre Brown
Louisa Brown
Margaret Bunke
Tatiana Bushey
Zachary Cardwell
Timothy Carey
Erin Carlon
William Cassidy
John Cearly
Carla Ceruzzi
Esther Cheung
Anne Chen
Elena Christakis
Katherine Chu
Kevin Chung
Sydney Cinalli
Donnohue Clarke
Meredith Contello
Whitney Cooper
Libba Cox
Susannah Cramer-Greenbaum
Rebecca Cumbermatch
Jeffrey Dike
Jake Eisenberg
Lou Fein
Luke Fein
Rachael Feinstein
Martha Foss
Ben Franceschi
Benjamin Bromberg Gaber
Amy Garlock
Colin Gast
Brett Gelnovatch
Eva George
Josh Glass
Dhara Goradia
Missy Grisnik
Ann Ha
Gregory Halpern
Bill Harper
Ben Harrison
Andrea Harsanyi
Noa Havilio
Ashley Heeren
Christina Hefferan
Jamie Hunt
Ivy Hurst
Cristina Ileana Suárez Iglesias
Mark Ingber
Tatsu Ikeda
Nicholas Jabs
Douglas Jack
Caroline James
Derek Johnson
Eric Jonash
Alexander Kalil
Sini Kampparri
Chris Karlson
Abby Klima
Peyton Knisley
Justin Kollar
Kaitlin Kurs
Michelle Laboy
David Lander
Cameron Lassiter
Marie Law
Karen Lee
Ryan Leidner
Ryan Lemmo
Gregory Logan
Perry Lubin
Asa Magdanz
Christopher Maj
Jamie Machek
Kelsey Margulies
David Martin
Clarinda Massengill
Evan Mathison
Ania Matteson
Victoria McGovern
Kenneth Mendez
Michael Meo
Paul Merril
Benjamin Meyers
Meghan Miklavic
Brittany Milas
Jonathan Miller
Matthew Moffitt
Dana Moore
Stephanie Morrison
Orion Morrison-Worrell
Thomas Moyles
John Mucciarone
Thomas Murdough
Adam Murfield
Christine Napolitano
Konstantinos Papadimitrako-poulos
Roberta Parritt
Eleonora Peretti
Yasmine Perez
Sarah Petri
Bill Pevear
Bret Pierson
Lisa Quackenbush
Rebecca Rahnlow
Reihaneh Ramezany
Courtney Richeson
Alan Ricks
Evan Rodriguez
Emma Rose
Michael Rose
Solomon Rosenthal
Matthew Ryan
Grace Rudolph
Murilo Santos
Phelan Shea
Reid Shea
Jussi Silliman
Caleb Silverman
William Simon
Fernando Diaz Smith
Ricardo Solar
Josh Sommers
Alexis Sparco
Sarah Spielman
Jessica Springer
Nathan Stanfield
James Steel
Rachael Stevens
Laurel Stone
Hope Strode
Mary Stuckert
Gerry Sullivan
David Suttle
Daina Swagerty
Katrina Szabo
Lynn Teng
Maryann Thompson
Jenny Tija
Eva Torontali-Gould
Jenny Tsia
Binu Tulachan
Ioana Urma
Sarah Vance
Alexandra Vanegas
Brenda Varela
Amy Vaugham
Jennifer Wang
Tamar Warburg
Jeremy Warms
Heather Weiler
Michael Wilcox
Michaela Wozniak
Jeff Vogel
Weishun Xu
Liwen Zhang

SELECTED BIBLIOGRAPHY

Amelar, Sarah. "Brooklyn Bridge Park Designers Transform a Defunct Shipping Complex and Reconnect a City with its Environment." *Architectural Record* 199, no. 1 (January 2011): 82–89.

Blanthorn, Jon Scott. "Parks and Regeneration." *Canadian Architect* 61, no. 11 (November 2016): 62–66. [Corktown Common Park]

Brown, Nell Porter. "Keeping It Green: Alumni Contribute to Sustainable Building." *Harvard Magazine* (November/December 2008): 24I–24L [Atrium School; Fayerweather Street House; Zero Impact House; Hinge House]

Campbell, Robert. "In this Spacious House, You're Always at One with Nature." *The Boston Globe* (January 26, 2006): N3. [Geothermal House]

Campbell, Robert. "The Power of Persuasion." *Architectural Record* 205, no. 8 (August 2017): 90–95. [Walden Pond Visitor Center]

Cannon, Robyn Roehm. "Finding the Light A Compact Cape Cod Cabin Abounds with Pleasant Views, Breezes & Sunshine." *Cabin Life* (August 2011): 48, 50–51. [Hilltop Glade]

Carter, Brian and Carla Swickenrath, eds. site/architecture: *Thompson and Rose Architects*. Ann Arbor: University of Michigan College of Architecture and Urban Planning. [Streitsview Barn; Leeper Studio Complex, Atlantic Center for the Arts]

Clarke, Gerald. "A Bend in the River Adapting to its site, a Massachusetts House Nestles into the Land." *Architectural Digest* 64, no. 6 (June 2007): 134–43, 217. [Westport Meadow House]

Conry, Jaci. "Enjoying the Outdoors from Inside." *The Boston Globe* (26 July 2012): 20–21G. [Fallen Leaves]

Conry, Jaci. "Modern Rustic." *The Boston Globe Magazine* (26 June 2011): 30–31. [The Small House]

Cunningham, Andrew. "From Fallen Leaves." *Cape Cod and Islands Home* (January 2006): 60–68, 70–71 [Fallen Leaves]

Darrow, Carl. "Barns East and West: Straitsview Barn." *Wood Design and Building* (Autumn 1997): 33–36.

De Gersdorff, Sascha. "No Place Like Home, Schoolhouse Rocks." *Boston Magazine* (April 2006): 106–11, 116, 118, 120, 122, 124, 126, 128–31. [Fayerweather Street House]

Eck, Jeremiah. "Geothermal House." *House in the Landscape: Siting Your Home Naturally*, 134–41. New York: Princeton Architectural Press, 2011.

Gangal, Sanjay. "Small House in Massachusetts by Maryann Thompson Architects." 30 November 2011. https://www10.aeccafe.com/blogs/arch-showcase/2011/11/30/small-house-in-massachusetts-by-maryann-thompson-architects/ [The Small House]

Garlough, Donna. "Where to Eat Now: 2010 Hot Seats." *Boston Magazine* (January 2010): 58. [Rialto Restaurant and Bar]

Guzowski, Mary. "Relationship to the Environment." *Daylighting for Sustainable Design*, 49–57. New York: McGraw-Hill, 2000. [Leeper Studio Complex, Atlantic Center for the Arts]

Hi-design International Publishing Co., Ltd., ed. "The Children's School." *Kindergarten Architecture II*, 286–95. Dalian, China: University of Technology Press, 2013.

Hoffer, Audrey. "Airy and Adaptable: Acorn Deck's Kit Homes Blur the Lines Between the Indoors and Outdoors." *The Washington Post* (15 November 2014). [Hinge House]

Humphries, Courtney. "Designing Green: Eco-friendly ideas take root in Boston." *Improper Bostonian* XV, no. 9 (3 May 2006): 34–37. [Geothermal House]

Jodidio, Philip. "Atlantic Center for the Arts." *Contemporary American Architects*, vol. IV, 180–85. Los Angeles: Taschen, 1998.

Ji-Hyun, Choi, et al. *New Space 10: Education & Culture*, 16–17, 112–113, 156–57. Seoul, S. Korea: Korea Archiworld Co., Ltd., 2009. [The Children's School]

Keates, Nancy. "A Modern Sunday Salon." *The Wall Street Journal* (18 February 2011): D8. [Traill Street House]

Kramer, Sibylle. "The Children's School, Stamford." *Schools Educational Spaces*, 80–83. Salenstein, Switzerland: Braun Publishing AG, 2010.

Kummer, Corby. "A Room of Her Own." *Boston Magazine* (July 2007): 131–33. [Rialto Restaurant and Bar]

Kunstel, Stacy. "Open Minded: A thought-provoking home on the outer Cape." *New England Home* (July/August 2013): 88–95. [Pamet Harbor House]

Lam, George. "Westport Meadow House." *House and Housing 101*, 104–07. Mississauga, Canada: designzens, Pace Publishing Ltd., 2012.

Lapiana, Maria. "Tiny Treasure." *New England Home* 15, no. 1 (September/October 2019): 66–71. [West Hill Guest House]

Levitt, Rachel. "Pushing the Eco Envelope." *Design New England* (January/February 2007): 72–81. [Geothermal House]

"Look to the Light." *Architecture: Innovative Spaces Shaping Global Design*, 117–18. Chicago: Alarm Press, 2013. [Temple Ahavat Achim]

Martin, Kyle and Nikki Mellado. "Geothermal House: Maryann Thompson Architects." *Inhabitat* (September 27, 2006). http//inhabitat.com/blog/2006/09/27/geohouse/

Martin, Tovah. "Into the Woods." *New England Home* (January 2023): 86–92. [Ocean Glen Cove]

"Maryann Thompson Architects." *Designscapes*, 63–69. London: B.B. Publications, 2017. [images of Bluff House, Foote School Science and Technology Center, The Children's School]

Morgan, William. "Structural Beauty." *Design New England* (November/December 2016): 58–60, 62–63. [International School of Boston Library]

Morgan, William. "Walden Pond Revised." *Design New England* (September/October 2017): 54, 56–59. [Walden Pond Visitor Center]

Moskow, Keith and Robert Linn. "Bluff House." *Martha's Vineyard Contemporary Living*, 44–51. New York: The Monacelli Press, 2010.

Moskow, Keith and Robert Linn. "The Oaks." *Martha's Vineyard New Island Homes*, 34–45. New York: The Monacelli Press, 2021.

Mulfinger, Dale. "One Big Room." *Back to the Cabin*, 218–23. Newtown CT: Taunton Press, 2013. [The Small House]

Murray, Erin Byers. "Jody Under Construction." *Boston Magazine* 49, no. 9 (September 2011): 98–103, 148–52, 154. [Trade Restaurant]

Pisor, Erik. "Sunny-Side South: Harnessing the Power of the Sun is the Key to Maryann Thompson Architects' Work at a Massachusetts Wildlife Sanctuary." *Green Building & Design* (September 2011): 92–93. [Farm Life Center, Drumlin Farm]

Postel, Louis. "Fallen Leaves." *Boston Magazine Home & Garden* (Fall 2006): 78–85.

Reed, Douglas, and Gary Hilderbrand. *Visible/Invisible: Landscape Works of Reed Hilderbrand*, 150–57, 297, 270–76. New York: Metropolis Books, 2012. [Leventritt Garden, Arnold Arboretum; Westport Meadow House]

Restuccia, Paul. "'Green House Effect." *Boston Herald* (27 October 2008): 27. [Hinge House]

Rooney, E. Ashley. "Maryann Thompson Architects." *Contemporary Boston Architects*, 163–71. Atglen PA: Schiffer Publishing, Ltd., 2012. [Bluff House; Hilltop Glade]

Rooney, E. Ashley. "Westport Meadow House." *Asian Influenced Architecture and Design*, 18–19, 173. Atglen PA: Schiffer Publishing Ltd, 2010.

Schibsted, Evantheia. "The Lean, Green Schoolhouse." *Edutopia* (April/May 2009): 50, 52, 54.

Schiffer, Loryn Wilson. "Fallen Leaves, Martha's Vineyard." *United By Design: Homes of Cape Cod, Martha's Vineyard, and Nantucket*, 221–35, rear cover. Atglen PA: Schiffer Publishing, Ltd., 2012.

Scott, Sarah. "The Children's School, New Canaan." *Architecture for Children*, 184–85. Camberwell, Australia: ACER Press, 2010.

Sharkey, Lisa and Paul Gleicher. "Simply Modern." *Dreaming Green*, 102–11 New York: Clarkston Potter, 2008. [Zero Impact House]

Shartan, Emily. "Greener Pastures: Architect Maryann Thompson designs a home in Easton, Massachusetts, that puts the environment first." *Design New England* (March/April 2008): 102–07. [Zero Impact House]

Silverberg, Michael. "The Glass Lab." *Metropolis* (February 2007): 84. [Broad Institute]

Slade, Rachel. "Arty in the Back." *Boston Home* (Spring 2017): 88, 94–97. [Smoketree House]

Snoonian, Deborah. "Reed Hilderbrand and Maryann Thompson Join Forces for the New Leventritt Shrub and Vine Garden in Boston." *Architectural Record* 193, no. 10 (October 2005): 124–27.

Stein, Karen. "Project Diary." *Architectural Record* 185, no. 6 (June 1997): 98–111. [Leeper Studio Complex, Atlantic Center for the Arts]

Stein, Karen. "Thompson and Rose's Equipment Building in Rural Washington State Demonstrates that there can be Elegance in Utility." *Architectural Record* 186, no. 6 (June 1998): 102–07. [Straitsview Barn]

Strahan, David. "Westport Meadow House." *Contemporary Villas*, 174–79. Atglen PA: Schiffer Publishing, Ltd., 2011.

Taylor, Tess. "Scientific Advancement: A David Small Installation promotes the use of the Broad Institute to the man on the street." *Metropolis* 266, no. 7 (March 2007): 62.

Thompson, Jessica Cargill. "Thompson and Rose Architects: Atlantic Center for the Arts." *40 Architects Under 40*, 492–95. Köln, London, Madrid, New York, Paris, Tokyo: Taschen, 2000.

Thompson, Maryann. "Egret Meadow House" and "The Oaks." Brian G. Carabet, ed., *The Modern Residence*, 443–48. Dallas: Intermedia Publishing, 2020.

Thompson, Maryann. "Nostalgic Ventures." *Architecture+* no. 11 (2006): 100–01. [Leventritt Garden Pavilion, Arnold Arboretum]

Thompson, Maryann. "Maryann Thompson, Cambridge, Massachusetts, USA." Center 16: "Latitudes: Architecture in the Americas," Vol 1 (University of Texas, Austin, 2012): 138–51.

Thompson, Maryann. "Polly Hill Arboretum." David Andreu Bach, ed., *Wood: Cozy Interiors for Timeless Living Spaces*, 156–60. Barcelona: boog publishing, 2024.

Thompson, Maryann. "Walden Pond Visitor Center" and "The Foote School Science and Technology Center." David Andreu Bach, ed. *Wood: Living and Working*, 122–31. Barcelona: booq publishing, 2019.

Thompson, Maryann. "Westport Meadow House." George Lam, ed. *House and Housing* 101, 104–07. Mississauga, Canada: designzens, Pace Publishing Ltd., 2012.

Thompson, Maryann. "Westport Meadow House" and "Geothermal House." Montse Barràs, ed., *Contemporary House Design*, 294–311. Cologne and London: daab gmbh, 2009.

Thompson, Maryann and Charles Rose. "Designer's Diary: Imagining Art in the Florida Jungle." *INSITE 3*, no. 4 (March 1994): 18–19.

Trulove, James Grayson. "Geothermal House Tracking the Sun." *The New Wood House*, 42–53. New York: Bulfinch Press, 2005..

Trulove, James Grayson. "Geothermal Residence" and "The Green House." *New Sustainable Homes: Designs for Healthy Living* 60–71, 130–39. New York: Collins Design Press, 2006. [Geothermal House, Zero Impact House]

Tucker, Lindsay. "Paradise Found." *Boston Home* (Spring 2013): 88–95. [Bluff House]

Uffelen, Chris Van. "Outdoor Classroom and Vine Trellises." *Collection Landscape Architecture*, 16–17. (Berlin, Germany: Verlaghaus Braun, 2009). [Leventritt Garden Pavilion, Arnold Arboretum]

Wagner, Joyce. "Inviting the Outside In: Visitor's Center, Polly Hill Arboretum, West Tisbury." *Martha's Vineyard Home & Garden* (Fall/Winter 2006–07): 28–35.

White, Clark. "Surf & Safari: A storied sportsmen's club on the Vineyard is re-imagined to provide adventure for a new generation." *Cape Cod Home* (Summer 2020): 72–79. [Watcha Pond House]

IMAGE CREDITS

Iwan Baan: 14, 72.
Jeremy Bitterman: 6, 10, 11, 52, 55, 56, 57, 58, 59, 60, 61, 62, 64, 98, 103, 117, 184, 185, 186, 193.
Leigh Chodas: 65, 66, 67, 116, 125.
Chuck Choi: 2, 5, 7, 8, 9, 12, 13, 18, 19, 28, 34, 35, 37, 38, 39, 40, 50, 51, 68, 70, 71, 73, 74, 75, 76, 82, 83, 84, 96, 97, 100, 101, 102, 105, 106, 107, 108, 109, 110, 113, 114, 115, 118, 119, 122, 127, 130, 131, 135, 140, 141, 142, 149, 150, 151, 154, 155, 156, 161, 162, 163, 166, 167, 183, 187, 190,, 191, 192, 194, 196, 197, 198.
Caroline Constant: 133, 152, 160, 195.
Scott Frances: 93, 94, 95, 203.
Mark Fairstein: 17.
Anton Grassi: 23, 24, 25, 26, 41, 43, 46, 47, 89, 111.
Greg Halpern: 134.
Millicent Harvey: 202, 205, 207.
Andrea Jones: 3.
Sabrina Cole Quinn: 164, 165.
Hyung Suk Lee: 104.
Stephen Lee: 137, 199, 200.
Eric Luciano: 173, 174, 175.
Charles Mayer: 128.
Scott Norsworthy: 15, 16, 22, 153.
Sabrina Cole Quinn: 164, 165.
Heath Robbins: 123, 171, 172.
Andreas Stavropolous: 204.
Brian Sytnyk: 201. [© Brian Sytnyk / Masterfile]
Maryann Thompson Architects: 29, 30, 90, 91, 120, 132, 138, 139, 148, 178.
Thompson and Rose: 126.
Stefen Turner: 48, 182.
Alan Ward: 206.
Peter Vanderwarker: 32, 112, 129, 158, 169, 170.
Sally Vargas: 176, 177, 179, 180, 181.
Private collection [reproduction strictly forbidden]: 69.

Acknowledgements

It has been a distinct pleasure to engage in extended conversations with Maryann Thompson on the trajectory of her practice—a process that has opened my eyes to the nuances of contemporary architectural production in significant new ways. I am especially grateful to MTA Principal Martha Foss for her careful attention to the details of the projects, her prompt attention to the many questions raised during the manuscript's production, and her work assembling the firm's credits. Without her discerning eye this book could never have happened. Of the various staff members who contributed time and energy to the book's production, six in particular stand out: Rei Ramezani, who aided in image selection, coordinated the photographic credits, and worked on obtaining image permissions; Ken Mendez, who established the standards for revising the drawings used in this publication and worked with Jeff Dike, Rei Ramezani, and Katie Chu to provide graphic consistency among the site plans, building plans, and diagrams; Zac Cardwell, who assisted with access to the MTA image database; and Tatiana Bushey, who compiled the draft bibliography and provided essential support in numerous ways.

Others have provided sage advice as the writing progressed: Michelle Laboy offered important insights into the projects she directed as a staff member at MTA; Michael Blier of Landworks Studio elaborated on his contribution to the Atrium School; Professor Casey-Lew Williams of Princeton University clarified his role at the Princeton Child Care Center; Ron McCoy and Alexander Karels assisted with permission to publish the latter project from Princeton University; and Jessie Harmes of Interra Consulting sought to obtain such permission from Novartis Pharmaceuticals. I am particularly grateful to Shantel Blakely, Terry Real, and Doug Reed for their individual contributions to this volume. Their essays have expanded my way of thinking about the work in ways that would not otherwise have been possible.

It has been especially rewarding to work on finalizing the book design with Chris Grimley of the design studio SIGNALS and the text with architecture critic and curator Mimi Zeiger. Chris has been meticulous in working out the complex layout issues associated with this project. His patience with our excessive demands has been particularly noteworthy. It was Chris who connected Maryann and I with Mimi Zeiger, who did a superb (and most welcome) job of editing the manuscript. My sincere thanks to Chris and Mimi for producing the interview with Maryann that concludes this volume. I have rarely had the opportunity to work with such engaging professionals.

ORO Editions
Publishers of Architecture, Art, and Design
Gordon Goff: Publisher

www.oroeditions.com
info@oroeditions.com

Published by ORO Editions

Author: Caroline Constant
With contributions by Shantel Blakely, Terry Real, and Doug Reed
Book Design: Chris Grimley
Project Manager: Jake Anderson

10 9 8 7 6 5 4 3 2 1 First Edition

ISBN: 978-1-961856-27-1

Prepress and Print work by ORO Editions Inc.
Printed in China

ORO Editions makes a continuous effort to minimize the overall carbon footprint of its publications. As part of this goal, ORO, in association with Global ReLeaf, arranges to plant trees to replace those used in the manufacturing of the paper produced for its books. Global ReLeaf is an international campaign run by American Forests, one of the world's oldest nonprofit conservation organizations. Global ReLeaf is American Forests' education and action program that helps individuals, organizations, agencies, and corporations improve the local and global environment by planting and caring for trees.